'This is a moving tribute to a brother's struggle with TBI; a harrowing account of the inadequacies of the service systems to provide the needed support, told through the eyes of a loving sister who is also a psychologist. It makes the book unique.'
- **Professor Grahame Simpson**, Brain Injury Rehabilitation Research Group, Ingham Institute, Australia

'This is a sad story and one that should never have needed to be told. I applaud the author for showing real bravery and writing an honest and frank account of the events which ultimately lead to tragedy.'
- **Hilary Dicks**, Former CEO of Headway Somerset, UK

'This book is essential for those in contact with people with brain injuries to help them develop insight into the complexity of this hidden disability. While not for the faint hearted, family members may find this book helpful to make sense of their own story, and trauma and loss they have experienced following brain injury.'
- **Charlotte Whiffin**, Senior Lecturer, Derby University, UK

'This book is a truly candid portrayal of life after brain injury, narrated with both personal and professional accounts. Highlighted is the stark reality and consequences individuals and their relatives face when services are not integrated and responsive.'
- **Freya Suffield**, Hospital Liaison Officer

'This book is an important addition to the range of ABI literature. It offers a unique rounded perspective – combining the immediate personal story of one man with ABI, with the wider context of his family story, alongside a professional analysis and perspective. It will be a vital source for families and professionals alike.'
- **Liz Simmons**, CEO Headway Somerset, UK

GW00644924

Life and Suicide Following Brain Injury

Life and Suicide Following Brain Injury tells the story of Tom, a 43-year-old man who acquired a brain injury from a road traffic accident at the age of 22. Tom survived but went on to take his own life 20 years later. This book tells Tom's story, as a vulnerable adult with mental health issues and long-term difficulties with substance misuse, from his early childhood through to his death.

In telling Tom's story, the author – a researcher in the brain injury field and Tom's sister – identifies the multiple suicide risk factors as well as the lack of understanding and inadequate service provision for people with complex needs following TBI. His story serves as a harrowing example of what can go wrong when timely intervention and support is not forthcoming, identifying a multitude of risk factors and possible points of intervention to improve care in the future.

This book provides insight to professionals and academics across health and social care in the risks of suicide associated with TBI. It also provides support for those who have experienced the grief of losing a survivor to suicide, or those struggling to support a survivor who is suicidal.

Alyson Norman, PhD, is a researcher in clinical psychology at the University of Plymouth's School of Psychology. Alyson has over 10 years experience of research in brain injuries and has personal experience as a family survivor of brain injury.

After Brain Injury: Survivor Stories
Series Editor: Barbara A. Wilson

This series of books is aimed at those who have suffered a brain injury, and their families and carers. Each book focuses on a different condition, such as face blindness, amnesia and neglect, or diagnosis, such as encephalitis and locked-in syndrome, resulting from brain injury. Readers will learn about life before the brain injury, the early days of diagnosis, the effects of the brain injury, the process of rehabilitation, and life now. Alongside this personal perspective, professional commentary is also provided by a specialist in neuropsychological rehabilitation, making the books relevant for professionals working in rehabilitation such as psychologists, speech and language therapists, occupational therapists, social workers and rehabilitation doctors. They will also appeal to clinical psychology trainees and undergraduate and graduate students in neuropsychology, rehabilitation science, and related courses who value the case study approach.

With this series, we also hope to help expand awareness of brain injury and its consequences. The World Health Organisation has recently acknowledged the need to raise the profile of mental health issues (with the WHO Mental Health Action Plan 2013–20) and we believe there needs to be a similar focus on psychological, neurological and behavioural issues caused by brain disorder, and a deeper understanding of the importance of rehabilitation support. Giving a voice to these survivors of brain injury is a step in the right direction.

The Invisible Brain Injury
Cognitive Impairments in Traumatic Brain Injury, Stroke and other Acquired Brain Pathologies
Aurora Lassaletta

Life After a Rare Brain Tumour and Supplementary Motor Area Syndrome
Awake Behind Closed Eyes
Alex Jelly, Adel Helmy, Barbara A. Wilson

Life and Suicide Following Brain Injury
A Personal and Professional Account
Alyson Norman

For more information about this series, please visit: www.routledge.com/ After-Brain-Injury-Survivor-Stories/book-series/ABI

Life and Suicide Following Brain Injury

A Personal and Professional Account

Alyson Norman

Routledge
Taylor & Francis Group

LONDON AND NEW YORK

First published 2020
by Routledge
2 Park Square, Milton Park, Abingdon, Oxon OX14 4RN

and by Routledge
52 Vanderbilt Avenue, New York, NY 10017

*Routledge is an imprint of the Taylor & Francis Group, an
informa business*

British Library Cataloguing-in-Publication Data
A catalogue record for this book is available from the
British Library

Library of Congress Cataloging-in-Publication Data
A catalog record has been requested for this book

ISBN: 978-1-138-57614-8 (hbk)
ISBN: 978-1-138-57615-5 (pbk)
ISBN: 978-1-351-27096-0 (ebk)

Typeset in Times New Roman
by Swales & Willis, Exeter, Devon, UK

I dedicate this book to Dave. You will always be in our hearts.

Contents

Foreword

The true meaning of life is to plant trees, under whose shade you do not expect to sit.

(Nelson Henderson)

Alyson Norman's book addresses difficult topic matters, ones that are often either left unspoken or are matters so imbued with pre-determined value judgements and meaning that they are less often picked apart and examined with an open mind.

Suicide, acquired brain injury, homelessness, mental health difficulties, substance use and the struggle to access suitable health and social care services, intertwine on these pages. Alyson unflinchingly uses her own and very personal experience of the death of her brother as a springboard for examining how and why his suicide happened, asking whether this was inevitable or was in fact predictable and, therefore, potentially avoidable. But this book is far more than an exercise in self-reflective autoethnography. It seeks to reposition the place of complex and difficult-to-serve people, people with multi-morbidity, people who do not fit into services ridden with eligibility criteria and boundaries that bear no relation to the reality of life with a severe brain injury.

None of us whose lives have been touched by suicide, personally or professionally, remain unchanged by the experience. We are left with questions that cannot and will not be answered. What this book does boldly and well is to use a solitary event, the death by suicide of one man, a man affected severely by brain injury, and reviews and unpicks this from multiple perspectives. In doing so a forensic light is shone not only on 'Tom' but on the family that surrounded him, the services he endeavoured to use or was provided with, and upon varying professional standpoints and opinions. Evidence from international research sits cheek by jowl on the page with details of an ordinary life. The empirical data of methodologically sound and peer reviewed articles intermeshes with the minutiae of life, the banal, the quotidian and the sometimes shocking. Commentary from those who knew Tom is woven together with the views of expert professional staff from the field. This is a brave and useful approach to take. Tom's life (and death) is transposed onto the research, and vice-versa, so that we may take away from this more than a story, we can question what we do, what we think and feel, and how we perhaps ought to look again at the most marginalised in our society. Like Kurosawa's masterpiece, the film *Rashomon*, this book allows for multiple subjective, alternative, and perhaps even contradictory versions of the same incident to be reviewed, and by doing this we are allowed to learn more.

However, this book is also far more than this. Peel away the empirical data, the referenced research on the impact of brain injury and of suicide, take away the expert commentary from across many professions, remove the analysis of the whole family system, erase the narrative that so fleshes this all out and makes it so visceral and real, and you are left with a love letter from a 12-year-old girl to her brain-injured brother. In the end this is all that counts. For as we struggle to generate terminologies and typologies, as we endeavour to understand the complex ways that humans act, be they brain injured or not, and as we seek evidenced-based ways of improving the responses we provide to people in crisis, it all comes down to love and people in the end. Nothing more.

Tom could never have known that after his suicide his story would be told. I like to think that the man who becomes very real to us as we read these pages, that unique, funny, gifted, difficult, challenging and tortured soul, would be pleased with his sister's efforts to create something that recognises his struggles but uses this to support others; crafting opportunities for learning from crisis and despair. This book takes a life lived on the periphery of society, a misunderstood life, a life too complex for simplistic responses, a life that could and should have been made better by appropriate interventions, and a death that was, in my view, ultimately preventable, and provides the reader with opportunities to reflect and learn. For that we owe Alyson and Tom, her wider family and those that contributed to this book a debt of gratitude.

Dr Mark Holloway

Acknowledgements

I would like to thank the people who have helped me to produce this account of Tom's life. Thank you to my mother and sister for agreeing to be part of the process and sharing their perspectives on Tom's life and death. Thank you too to all the professionals who have supported this book with their professional reflections: James Tonks, Angus Crutchfield, Wendy Copeman, Hilary Dicks, Louise Hawkins, Yasmin Drew and Jo Clark-Wilson. And a special thanks to Mark Holloway who provided a professional reflection and wrote the foreword to this book.

Finally, thank you to David Bennett and Alison Bacon for painstakingly reading drafts.

Chapter 1

An introduction to traumatic brain injury and suicidality

Acquired brain injury (ABI) is any event sustained during or after birth that results in an alteration to brain function (Headway UK, 2018a). The most common causes of ABI include illness or infection (e.g. meningitis, encephalitis, tumours), or injury (e.g. accidents, falls or assaults). This last cause is categorised as a subset of ABI, called traumatic brain injuries (TBIs). ABIs and TBIs can cause an array of difficulties with physical, emotional, behavioural and cognitive functioning. I am going to focus predominantly on TBI throughout this book, as my brother 'Tom' experienced a TBI in 1993 as a result of a car accident. Common physiological side effects include mobility impairments, difficulties with speech, sensory impairments and ongoing fatigue (Headway UK, 2018a). Emotional difficulties include anxiety and depression, an increased risk of developing psychosis and personality disorders, and wider changes to personality (Holloway, 2014). Behavioural side effects include irritability and aggression. Finally, cognitive difficulties include language impairments, attentional difficulties, impaired concentration, memory problems and executive impairments (Holloway, 2014). Executive impairments include difficulties with planning, problem solving, decision-making, and inhibiting and initiating behaviour (Maas et al., 2017). Executive impairment can also lead to a lack of insight into the level of disability the individual is experiencing (George & Gilbert, 2018).

There are approximately 350,000 new admissions for ABI every year in the UK, with an estimated two million people living with long-term disability associated with ABI (Headway UK, 2018a). Hospital admissions for TBI are approximately 156,000 per year in the UK (Headway UK, 2018a). TBI is the most common cause of long-term disability for an estimated 500,000 people in the UK (Maas et al., 2017). This highlights that for many ABI survivors, their disability will span a lifetime.

This long-term aspect of ABI brings with it a significant cost to the UK economy. A 2016 report concluded that TBI alone costs the UK economy £15 billion a year (Parsonage, 2016).

Although ABI and TBI are so common, literature has shown that knowledge about the impact of both is relatively limited among the general population (Linden & Boylan, 2010). While academic literature clearly identifies the life-long impact that TBI specifically can have on the lives of both patients and families (Langlois, Rutland-Brown & Wald, 2006), there is a dearth of information within the public domain (Linden & Boylan, 2010). The acute service provision for TBI is focused upon life-sustaining care and promoting physical recovery (Odumuyiwa et al., 2019), and many patients will go on to inpatient neurorehabilitation services where they will receive access to neurology, speech and language therapy (SALT), occupational therapy (OT), physiotherapy and neuropsychology (Silver et al., 2018). Yet, the literature suggests that despite this important care 'pathway', many health professionals working within acute care, and even within neurorehabilitation, have a limited understanding of the life-long nature of the impairments caused by TBI (Knight & Norman, 2017).

As this book unfolds, I will share my experiences of living alongside a man who experienced just such a life-long set of impairments and his ongoing battle with poor mental health and suicidal ideation. Before moving on to the personal account, I thought it was important to set TBI within the context of a long-term health condition and outline the evidence for the link between TBI and suicide, as captured in the academic literature.

From the point of discharge from rehabilitation or acute care, people with TBIs often experience a sense of being 'abandoned' by the health care system (Graff, Christensen, Poulsen & Egerod, 2017) and being unsupported by social care systems, leaving them unable to reintegrate into social and community contexts (Salter, Foley, Jutai, Bayley & Teasell, 2008). While some may receive good access to SALT, OT and physiotherapy within the community, this is the exception rather than the norm, with access to these services generally being poor or non-existent (UKABIF, 2018). Where provision is available, rehabilitation often takes the form of that provided by generic community practitioners rather than being provided by ABI specialist services (Odumuyiwa et al., 2019). This leads to high levels of unmet needs (Salter et al., 2008). This is further exacerbated by the cognitive impairments that are associated with TBI, which make it problematic for individuals to reintegrate back into the world of work or education post-injury – as few as 40% of survivors manage to return to work within two years (Van Velzen, Van Bennekom, Edelaar, Sluiter & Frings-Dresen, 2009). The impairments associated with TBI also limit a survivor's capacity to re-engage with their previous social networks, due to changes in personality, aggression or disinhibited behaviours, and emotional dysregulation (Salter et al., 2008). These impairments lead to a breadth of community and social integration needs that often lead to high levels of social deprivation (UKABIF, 2018). It is important to note that these needs are life-long and require a complex ongoing package of care to enable integration (Odumuyiwa et al., 2019). Such care packages are often not forthcoming due to a lack of availability and a lack of commissioning (UKABIF, 2018; Odumuyiwa et al., 2019; House of Lords, 2014).

Access to care packages and benefits are further limited by executive impairments associated with TBI. These 'hidden' disabilities often lead to a failure in receiving benefits, or the cessation of benefits, due to survivors lacking insight into the level of their impairments, forgetting appointments or struggling to navigate the complex systems associated with accessing care and benefits (Odumuyiwa et al., 2019; Moore, Wotus, Norman, Holloway & Dean, 2019). This ultimately increases the risk of social deprivation and can be further exacerbated by the poor financial decision-making and poor initiation of behaviour that can be associated with executive impairments. These behaviours may lead to individuals putting themselves at risk of homelessness through an inability to pay their bills, or by failing to keep their property in an adequate state of cleanliness (Moore et al., 2019; Norman, 2016). This leaves survivors at an increased risk of homelessness, with as many as 40% of the homeless population having sustained a TBI prior to becoming homeless (Oddy, Moir, Fortesque & Chadwick, 2012).

The literature on long-term integration following TBI paints a bleak picture. The emotional and behavioural difficulties associated with TBI can also lead to anxiety and depression in the population, even amongst those who had no previous pre-morbid history (Ponsford & Schönberger, 2010). Those with previous difficulties pre-injury often experience an exacerbation of symptoms. Substance misuse is also commonplace, with 60% of TBI survivors experiencing drug and alcohol problems, 25% of which will have had no pre-morbid history (Ponsford, Whelan-Goodinson & Bahar-Fuchs, 2007). Furthermore, the executive impairments associated with TBI can lead to impaired decision-making that is often associated with increased risk-taking behaviour (Moore et al., 2019). This behaviour can lead to school exclusion, for those of school age (Williams et al., 2010), and potential involvement with the police and prison service, often occurring through individuals getting caught up in theft or violent crime (Shiroma, Ferguson & Pickelsimer, 2012). TBI survivors have been found to be highly represented within the prison population.

Unsurprisingly, the long-term consequences of social deprivation and isolation, alongside an inability to cope with the myriad of post-injury neurological changes outlined above, often leads to a dramatic decrease in the quality of life for TBI survivors (Bay, Bonnie, Williams, Kirsch & Gillespie, 2002), and their families (Townshend & Norman, 2018; Holloway, Orr & Clark-Wilson, 2019). One possible consequence of this is an increased risk of suicide (Madsen, Erlangsen & Orlovska, 2018; Bahraini, Simpson, Brenner, Hoffberg & Schneider, 2013). These risk factors, in conjunction with neurological changes that can exacerbate suicidal ideation in and of themselves, mean that TBI survivors are approximately three times more likely to take their own lives than individuals who have not suffered a TBI (Madsen et al., 2018; Bahraini et al., 2013).

While the academic literature on TBI survivors tells us it is common to experience mental health problems, substance misuse, involvement in criminal activity, homelessness and suicidal ideation, there are few clinical case studies that demonstrate all these factors in quite the same way as that of Tom. Tom was the subject of a Safeguarding Adults Review published in 2017. He experienced all of the above difficulties and, as a result, took his own life in July 2014. Tom was also my brother. From my perspective of both a family member and an academic psychologist with a specialist research interest in TBI, I write the account that follows in order to shed some light on how Tom reached the point of ending his life. I tell this tale in order to highlight the life-long nature of TBI and the vulnerability of adults with TBI who are left to fend for themselves in the community. I will also try to capture examples of best practice when working with TBI survivors in the community, in order to demonstrate how professionals may be able to reduce the likelihood of suicide among the TBI population. Finally, I give this account in order to outline the effect it has had on my family.

The book will take you, the reader, through the journey of Tom's life, starting with his life prior to his road traffic accident in 1993, through to his life immediately prior to his death in 2014. The book also outlines the experiences of myself, my mother 'Betty' and my sister 'Anna', through Tom's life and the aftermath of his suicide.

The personal nature of this account hopefully provides depth to Tom's story, with a view to increasing awareness of the risks of suicide post-TBI and improving the support offered by professionals to both survivors and families. It is hoped that this book will provide a useful insight to professionals across health and social care settings, as well as being a source of support for families going through similar circumstances.

Chapter 2

Growing up with a brain injury

Tom was my brother but, being 10 years older than me, I do not feel I really knew him much as a child. Tom had his accident in December 1993 when I was only 12 years old. I do not have many memories of him from when I was little and he moved out of home when I was about nine years old. Ours was not a happy family, which in part led Tom down the route he would ultimately take. We also had a complex family make-up and so I have included, in Figure 2.1, a genogram outlining the key members of our family and their relationships to one another. My main memories of him are from when he was about 16 years old and onwards. I idealised him as most little sisters idealise their big brothers. I thought he was cool and great fun to be around but even then he was a troubled young man with mental health difficulties. However, none of that mattered to me as a small child. All I saw was a boy who loved to give his little sister hugs and kisses and who always wanted to spend time with her no matter how old he got.

Nevertheless, my perspective as a child is only part of who Tom was. This chapter tells the life of Tom prior to his accident in 1993. While this may not seem directly relevant to the story, Tom's early years played an important role in who he would become, partly due to the nature of our family environment but also due to the multitude of injuries that Tom sustained throughout his childhood.

Over the years, our professional understanding of the impact of 'mild' traumatic brain injuries (mTBIs) has increased. While this area of research is still contentious, we understand that even mild injuries and concussions can have a significant impact on the day-to-day functioning of an individual (Wiebe, Cornstock & Nance, 2011). Further, recent literature has identified a negative cumulative effect of multiple head injuries that can lead to a host of difficulties

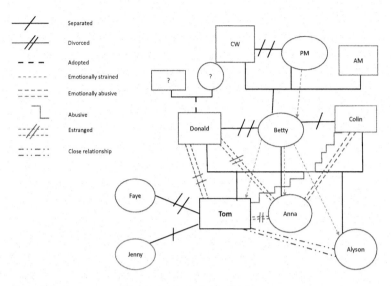

Figure 2.1 Genogram of Tom's family and relationships

with impaired function (Sariaslan, Sharp, D'Onofrio, Larsson & Fazel, 2016). These include emotional dysregulation, executive impairment and behavioural difficulties (Sariaslan et al., 2016). Tom experienced four such 'minor' injuries in childhood at the ages of 3, 8, 14 and 17. Clinical teams did not identify the significance of these multiple head injuries. In fact, they were not even noted by us as a family.[1] Yet they could have gone some way to explaining the high levels of depression, suicidality and risk-taking behaviour that characterised Tom's adolescent years.

Due to the limited memories I have of Tom from his younger years, I have pieced together this account from stories shared with me by my mother Betty,[2] my sister Anna, my father 'Colin' and from Tom himself before he died. There are also other accounts from Tom's friends who knew him during this time. It must be noted here that these accounts and events may not be wholly accurate, but are instead taken from the perspectives of the individuals who were witness to them.

Tom was born on the 19 March 1971 in Surrey. He was the eldest of three children. His sister Anna was born 18 months later and his youngest sister (me) was born 10 years later in 1981. Tom's mother's account of his early childhood highlights the difficulties within the family home. Both Betty and Donald (Tom's father) had previous family difficulties that may not have made them 'ideal' parents. Betty came from a broken home; her parents divorced when she was 12 years old and she and her brother were raised by their mother and step-father, both of whom were cold and emotionally unavailable. Donald was an illegitimate child born in protestant Ireland and was placed in foster care. He was raised by unloving and uncaring foster parents, which led him to run away to sea at 16 years of age. He was an ambitious man with a desire to do well for himself. He eventually settled in the Civil Service where he met Betty who was also working there.

In 1973, Donald was offered the opportunity to relocate to a job in Glasgow. The family had no money to buy a property near London, so took the chance to get on the property ladder. In 1974, at the age of three, Tom experienced his first encounter with mTBI when he was knocked down by a car. Tom had taken an interest in the mechanical work a local neighbour had been doing in his garage and had gone across the road to watch him. Once Tom had seen all he wanted he went to go back across the street to the family home. Unfortunately, neither his parents nor the neighbour were observing him and he stepped out between two parked cars and was hit by a passing vehicle. Tom was taken to the local hospital where he was diagnosed with a head injury.[3]

The family lived in Glasgow for three years until the weather in Scotland drove them south again. Tom was suffering regularly with coughs and colds and it was decided that a warmer climate may help his overall health. It was at that time that the family settled in Somerset, where Tom started primary school. Betty reflects that Tom was a bright child from early on in his schooling. He was ahead of his classmates in most subjects, particularly Maths. The school seemed unable to accommodate his advanced abilities and he was often left to his own devices during classes as he had quickly exhausted the stage books for Maths, even those above his level.

Tom experienced another head injury in 1979, at 8 years of age, when he fell off his push bike at speed. This incident was recorded in Tom's medical notes as a minor head injury, but Betty was unable to remember any details about the event. Anna recalls how Tom had gone over the handlebars of his bike and had 12 stitches in his face – in the top of his forehead and down his cheek, under his nose and his chin.

During Tom's time at primary school, Betty and Donald's marriage started to go badly wrong. In an attempt to find something to work on together, they moved again within the local area, taking on the restoration of an old Georgian property. Rather than bringing the family together, however, the building project had quite the reverse effect and Betty and Donald's marriage continued to deteriorate. It was during this time that Betty started a relationship with Colin; a local builder employed to work on the restoration project. During this time Tom was apparently reasonably settled, despite the difficulties with his parents' relationship. He had an avid interest in sports; he was a keen swimmer and enjoyed Judo. In 1979 Betty moved out of the marital home and in 1980 moved in with Colin, along with Tom and Anna.

The following year, Tom's youngest sister was born (me), daughter of Betty and Colin. At this point Tom's life started to change dramatically. He was soon to start secondary school, his parents had separated, and the tensions within the family home between Tom and Colin were high. Colin was an unwell man, experiencing dramatic mood swings brought on by a rare thyroid condition, and Tom's behaviour was increasingly unruly. The introduction of a half-sister on to the scene only exacerbated the tensions further. Meanwhile, Tom's father, Donald, had met another woman and remarried. Betty describes Tom's relationship as continuing to be close to Donald after he remarried, but both Anna and Tom paint a somewhat different picture. Neither Tom nor Anna felt welcomed into this new family home, leaving Tom to feel somewhat abandoned. Tom felt rejected by his father and, to some extent, by our mother too, leaving him feeling isolated and unloved.[4]

Despite the family tensions, Tom gained a scholarship to a public school in the neighbouring town. Tom was intelligent and more than capable of excelling at public school. At secondary school he made lots of new friends. Tom once told me that at this time he felt a sense of relief; that he was no longer being rejected by those around him. But these were not real friends; Tom was a poor boy moving in a rich man's world and he did not fit in. To those who have never been in this situation it may seem surprising that a boy like Tom would not revel in private school education, but the children who attend such schools are, for the most part, wealthy. Their lifestyles were so different from someone like Tom's that he never could fit in. Our family was not from a wealthy background. With Colin's deteriorating health due to his thyroid condition, he was forced to give up his work as a builder. This resulted in the family cutting back on all 'non-essential' items. By this point, Tom's behaviour had started to unravel. There are many possible causes for this; our family home environment was not a happy or supportive one, Tom had already sustained two head injuries that are associated with increased risk-taking behaviour (Sariaslan et al., 2016) and he was a 'poor boy' studying alongside children from wealthy families. Any one of these factors could have led to problems but the combination of them all was catastrophic.

Not long after starting secondary school, Tom was caught shoplifting. This was not a major offence but was the start of something much more serious. This was followed by a series of infringements of school rules, including bringing a fish hook into school that resulted in a fellow pupil's school uniform being torn. This ultimately led to the school 'asking Tom to leave', although Betty states that he was not actually excluded. By this point Anna had also gained a scholarship to the local public school and Betty was able to convince the school to allow Tom to transfer under the 13+ scheme, on the provision that any further bad behaviour would lead to an exclusion. It was during his time at this school, in 1985, that Tom sustained his third head injury. Again, Betty cannot recall any specific details about this event, but Tom's medical records state that he was admitted to hospital having sustained a concussion injury from a head injury. Betty suggested that this was a sport-related injury from playing cricket and Anna similarly states that the accident happened because Tom was hit with a cricket ball. She recalls that he had to spend time in the hospital for his concussion, which she believes to have been two days.

It was not long after this that Tom's behaviour led to him being excluded from the school and being enrolled in the local comprehensive. From here, Tom started engaging in increasingly risky behaviours including substance misuse and criminal activity. During this time he was caught breaking and entering into a local factory, leading to an appearance in juvenile court and being assigned a social worker whose role was to work with the family as a whole. Betty recalls that she was aware that he was using drugs during this time but was unsure what drugs he was involved with and to what extent. Anna, too, was aware that Tom was engaged in drug use but did not fully know the situation. Colin, however, has since reflected that he was aware of the situation and had reported it to Betty on numerous occasions. He had even identified that Tom had engaged in heroin use.

Despite the involvement of social services, the family situation did not improve. There was no psychological support or intervention. The focus seemed to be purely on observing and attending meetings. Colin was regularly verbally and, at times, physically abusive to Tom, and Tom spent increasingly less time in the house. Donald offered to have Tom come to live with him. This did not happen as Anna and Tom wanted to stay together and Donald would not have both of them. Tom did not bother to attend school and passed his GCEs on his intelligence alone. He went on to become a mechanic's apprentice at a nearby garage, but his interest in work was minimal. It was when Tom was 16 years old that Colin decided to leave the family home.

From the age of about 16 years onwards, Tom was rarely in the house. He had developed a love of motorbikes and, in the months just before his 16th birthday, he was given the opportunity to purchase a small motorbike. Betty agreed on the provision that the bike was to remain locked in the garage until he was old enough to ride it and had taken his test. One day when Betty was at work, Colin gave Tom the key to the garage, not realising what he had in mind. Tom took the motorbike out for a spin and ended up crashing it into a car.[5] This was to be the start of an ongoing relationship with motorbikes. In 1988, Tom had yet another head injury, this time due to a road traffic accident. Tom often rode his motorbike at high speeds. He loved motorbikes and was never happier than when he was out riding fast. On this particular day, he failed to brake quickly enough when the car in front of him stopped suddenly. His bike hit the back of the car at around 80 miles an hour and he somersaulted over the top, hitting his head on the roof of the car as he went. The force of this impact was so severe that it cracked the crash helmet he was wearing. This was one of many motorbike accidents but, thankfully, the only one that ended in a hospital admission. He was diagnosed with a 'minor' head injury and discharged from hospital.

Betty then met a new partner, 'Eric'. The relationship between Tom and Eric was no better than that between Tom and Colin, with the possible exception that Tom spent so little time in the house that the pair rarely had a chance to clash. Yet, there were still tensions. Even for me, as a very young child, I remember many arguments between my mum and my brother, and sometimes between him and Eric. In 1990, Betty married Eric and Tom was there to give her away, despite his feelings towards Eric. It was also in that year that Tom left home. One day Tom came home with his motorbike and offered me (a girl of 9 years of age) a ride on the front. I remember earnestly accepting. He put the spare crash helmet on my head, sat me in front of him and then rode up and down the lane at the back of our house. He did go fast, and certainly too fast for the conditions of the road with a young child on board, but at that age it all seemed very fun. Betty on the other hand did not agree. She flew into a rage on finding out and told Tom to leave the family home for good. She has since stated she does not remember saying this to him, but I can still remember very clearly standing in the kitchen of our house screaming at her to let him stay. Tom was 19 years of age.

Initially Betty helped set Tom up in a bedsit in the local town with a group of his friends. Tom moved between a few different bedsits before moving into lodgings with a chaplain from one of the local colleges. The chaplain seemed to want to support Tom and for a period of time acted almost like a father figure towards him. Betty recalls that on one occasion the pair took a motorbike trip to Loch Lomond. During this time, Tom had a steady job (as a cartographic trainee on undersea mapping) and seemed to be doing well for himself. Yet, this was not to last. In December 1991, Betty, Eric and I moved to the town where Tom was living and during the same month Tom and Anna's father, Donald, died of cancer. Neither Tom nor Anna had much contact with their father for several years but one can only imagine that this had some effect on Tom. Tom had started engaging with drug and alcohol community services. At some point during 1992, the lure of criminality (stealing cars, police chases, ram raiding and burglaries) and ongoing substance misuse proved too strong for Tom and he ended up homeless from his bedsit, sleeping rough on the streets of Exeter and in the hills near our home. Tom spent six months living rough and during this time was arrested for begging in the street. The family became aware of this when Tom appeared on the doorstep asking for a place to stay. He was able to get a place at the local homeless shelter. During this time, we rarely saw Tom. He would sometimes come back for visits but this was very infrequent. Tom was unhappy at his lot in life and although he knew that his substance misuse was not helping him, he found it difficult to give it up.

It was during 1992, at the age of 21, that Tom had his first experience of attempted suicide. By this time he was heavily engaged in heroin use. He and his friends were using when Tom decided to take an overdose of heroin. One of Tom's friend's put him in a wheelbarrow, pushed him to the local hospital and left him outside the Accident & Emergency department for treatment.[6] Early in 1993, Tom was arrested for being drunk and was admitted to hospital again with alcohol toxicity. He discharged himself but was readmitted later that day having had a suspected seizure. He survived these incidents and then re-engaged with drug and alcohol misuse services for support.

Tom's brief encounter with drug and alcohol misuse services did prompt a small change in his behaviour. By the middle of 1993 Tom had been dry for several months, but he was still mentally unwell. He was struggling with motivation and was still suicidal. He had started to self-neglect and the verdict of the GP at the time was that he was 'not amenable to medical help.'[7] There were continuous issues and in October 1993 Tom was arrested for stealing a car. He appeared in court in December and was issued with a fine. Despite this, between the time of his arrest and the court hearing, he did start a part time job and also started a relationship with a girl named Faye. For the first time in a very long time, Tom seemed vaguely happy and settled.

Reflections

Personal reflections

The following chapter will discuss the accident that led to Tom's diagnosed TBI. Yet, this chapter already provides a case example of the information outlined in Chapter 1. Tom's early years capture eloquently these links in a sad and poignant tale. His early life was punctuated by mental health difficulties, particularly depression. While TBI is unlikely to have been the only cause (with family breakdown and discord, and his school experiences as an outsider, being equally important contributors), Tom's case does highlight the link between TBI and an increased risk of developing mental health difficulties (Ponsford & Schönberger, 2010). Furthermore, Tom's spiral into substance abuse is also common amongst those who have sustained TBIs (Ponsford et al., 2007). His adolescent risk-taking behaviour is characteristic of executive impairment brought on by frontal lobe injury, which may have been sustained in his earlier injuries. Injuries in childhood can substantially change the functioning of the brain in many unique ways, based upon age, site and severity of the injury (Catroppa et al., 2017). Impairments caused by injuries in childhood are not always determinable immediately; difficulties may become apparent only in adolescence once social and learning environments become more complex (Casey, Giedd & Thomas, 2000; Savage, 2010) and the development of the frontal regions of the brain accelerates (around the time of secondary school onwards (Gogtay et al., 2004)). Tom's inability to retain work and accommodation are also identified as potential consequences of TBI (Oddy et al., 2012; Van Velzen et al., 2009), as are increases in criminal activity (Shiroma et al., 2012; Williams et al., 2010). Finally, Tom's suicidal ideation has been noted in studies of those post-injury (Bahraini et al., 2013; Madsen et al., 2018).

While it will never be possible to know whether the mTBIs sustained by Tom in his early childhood were responsible for these issues, Tom's profile is certainly familiar to those in the field. I still remember very vividly the evening that I was told about the previous injuries that Tom had sustained early in childhood. It was after his death and during the process of his Safeguarding Adults Review. The chair of the review came to talk to us as a family and disclosed what she had found from Tom's medical records. I remember going numb. I had always put Tom's issues down to poor family background and often wondered what led him to go down such a destructive path whilst my sister and I, despite having similar experiences, had not. This meeting clarified things for me; all this time, despite my professional knowledge, I had been 'flying blind'. I was without the key facts that I needed to piece the puzzle together. It occurred to me that our understanding of the events in our lives are based around the narratives we have about them. Mine had always been one of a brother who was 'wayward' and 'nonconformist'. These statements are still true but my reasoning about the causes of those behaviours has now changed; he was a brain injury survivor far before we realised. My reflection now, looking back on this information, is that perhaps if my family had understood the impact of such a series of events on someone's functioning, then perhaps Tom's life would have turned out differently. Support at this point from a child or educational psychologist may have proven useful for identifying Tom's underlying issues and enabling us, as a family, to cope.

As well as the uncertainty that will forever remain around the role that Tom's early head injuries played in his behaviour, the role of his familial life events and head injuries are difficult to untangle when considering his risk factors for suicide (see Case study 1.1 and Professional reflections 1.1–1.2). Tom as an adolescent was experiencing depression, although never formally diagnosed. This is, of course, a risk factor for suicide. Tom had also tried to take his life on one occasion prior to his 'main' head injury, also suggesting a pre-morbid risk factor. Yet, it is unclear how much these mental health problems were a result of the previous injuries and how much they were linked to other life events. Moreover, suicide and brain injury are so intrinsically linked that it is difficult to establish a clear directional relationship between the two; studies have identified that adverse childhood events (ACEs) are more likely to lead to head injuries (Ma et al., 2017), and both have been implicated in an increased risk of suicide (Madsen et al., 2018; Thompson, Kingree & Lamis, 2019); cases of brain injury have been reported in those who have attempted suicide and been left with hypoxic or traumatic injuries as a result (Jawaid, Amalnath & Subrahmanyam, 2017); studies have highlighted the post-injury mental health issues that can lead to an increased risk of suicide (Bahraini et al., 2013).

Case study 2.1: 'Harriet'

Harriet was in her twenties when she tried to take her own life through a drug and alcohol overdose. Harriet was found unconscious and unresponsive and was taken to the Accident and Emergency unit for resuscitation. Harriet remained unconscious for over 12 hours. The paramedics suspect Harriet had experienced oxygen deprivation to her brain prior to their arrival and had experienced inevitable brain injury from the cocktail of drugs she had consumed. She was in intensive care for 24 hours and then admitted to a high dependency unit, and subsequently transferred to an acute psychiatric unit.

After the suicide attempt Harriet reported a period of apraxia and aphasia. She also reported ongoing difficulties with her memory and displayed signs of executive impairment including poor planning, organisation, initiation and a lack of insight into her own disabilities.

Prior to her suicide attempt Harriet had experienced a multitude of ACEs (a range of negative childhood experiences, such as bullying, sexual abuse and neglect); an abusive childhood consisting of childhood sexual abuse from the ages of 5 years to 9 years of age, numerous counts of bullying through later childhood and adolescence, family neglect and reports of a mother who was 'uncaring' and unresponsive to her needs. Harriet started social drinking when she was in her teens and again experienced sexual abuse.

These adverse childhood experiences left Harriet feeling worthless and unloved. She became a drug addict and struggled with mental health problems, including bulimia, anxiety, depression and borderline personality disorder. Harriet reported feeling that nobody cared for her and everyone thought she was a 'useless' human being. Her drug addiction was then revealed to her parents who evicted her from the family home. It was while homeless that Harriet took her overdose. These ACEs led Harriet to choose the path of suicide. It was then the act of this attempted suicide that led her to experience a brain injury that further exacerbated her already complex circumstances.

Prior to Harriet's overdose, she had experienced a succession of smaller, yet potentially significant traumatic brain injuries. Harriet's experiences with bullies led her to experience a head injury at the age of 12, and she was also assaulted at the age of 18. At 16 years of age, and again at 22 years of age, Harriet fell from a horse and was knocked unconscious. These ongoing incidents of head injury show clearly the interplay between ACEs and head injury (Adshead, Norman & Holloway, 2019) and suicidality, which in turn exacerbated Harriet's brain injury.

Professional reflection 1.1: Reflections from James Tonks, paediatric neuropsychologist

Tom's injury history, his life at home, and this tragic set of circumstances are a stark reminder of the effects of multiple injuries to the brain in a context where there are other overlapping and poorly understood variables.

Tom experienced multiple adverse interpersonal events, involving abandonment and abuse whilst with various caregivers. This continued over an extended period of time. These variables would have increased his risk of experiencing difficulties with emotional and behavioural dysregulation without injury to the brain. As a result of Tom's own socio-emotional development in an unpredictable, stressful and sometimes dangerous environment, across the span of his childhood and early adolescence, I do not doubt that there was potential that Tom would have developed chronically altered expectations and perceptions. However, there is some indication that Tom was intelligent. This was likely a protective factor. I consider that, over-time, the composite effects of four repeat blows to the head reduced his propensity to down-regulate and retain control over his somewhat raw emotional condition. This is likely how I might formulate my understanding of Tom's difficulties, had I met him in a clinical setting.

There are neuroprotective treatments that are available today, which would not have been available as early as 1974. I believe that in those days an ambulance was little more than a van with a bed in it, compared to the mobile emergency units we have today. I think our understanding of repeat mild brain injury is still evolving by comparison to medical and technological advances in acute treatment. I think, even today, there would be a risk that his repeat concussive history could be overlooked or not recognised as significant. Children who suffer brain injury under the age of 10 are at significant risk of later developing problems with mood regulation, social understanding and empathy. Their emotional distress levels often equal those of children accessing the Child and Adolescent Mental Health Service (CAMHS). Adults with a history of brain injury that was never mediated with psychological treatments are twice as likely to develop mental health disorders. Tom's injury would have meant that he was likely to experience a greater degree of peer isolation and difficulties in friendships, and his challenging behaviour would have increased the already stress-burdened relationships within the home. Tom's criminality in his later years, and his involvement with drugs, is no less linked to brain injury. Young offenders with a history of three or more concussions typically repeat offend. Studies of prison inmates with a brain injury history show that they will be more likely to be in custodial systems whilst still children and they are twice as likely to self-medicate with cannabis every day. The effects of THC often only magnify poor self-regulatory behaviour. There are many examples of adults who have survived a troubled childhood with amazing resilience. There are many more examples of adults who, after brain injury of some kind, sadly do not.

How would I try to fix this? I would have attempted to build protective systems around Tom. How could we keep him engaged in education? Could we improve his family function with support? Could we target peer relationships as a form of intervention? How could we increase his social resources and improve upon his sense of identity and self-concept? In the end, he felt alone and did not feel good about himself or the world. He did not come to this view quickly, rather the evidence around him convinced him of this over time. The opportunities to prevent his views from forming were missed many years before.

What was his personal story? Would it have helped him to know that the brain injury could trick him into thinking and acting-out in certain ways? If you are familiar with the forces that can move you, you can adjust your balance. I would have made him aware of his triggers, high-risk situations and the early warning signs that things were going wrong. We would have agreed a plan of what he could do and how others could help him/how he wanted to be treated. We would have played back the real-time situations that had gone wrong to look to see if we could identify the decision points, and where different decisions or further support could have helped.

I do not know if supporting Tom in these ways would ultimately mean that he would not end his life. I do consider that the absence of support meant that the likelihood of such an outcome was greatly increased.

Professional reflection 1.2: Reflections of Angus Crutchfield, systemic psychotherapist

> *In the context of childhood brain injury, we understand that vertical-brain networks regulate movement, thinking, emotional responding, learning and emotional behaviour and that following brain injury, these networks are damaged leading to disorganised, dysregulated functioning.*
>
> (Byard & Gosling, 2013)

From infancy, family circumstances were stacked against a smooth developmental trajectory for Tom. The familial backdrop was one of marital disharmony, multiple marital breakdowns, the emotional numbness of his mother, geographical displacement and, perhaps most relevantly for Tom, the intersection of his being a child from an impoverished background associating with 'posh kids' as a result of his towering academic strength in maths, securing his scholarship status at a school that almost exclusively serves the fortunate children of the wealthy. Much like a homemade pie is liable to collapse without a strategically placed pie-funnel to support the unformed pastry whilst the ingredients are baking, it struck me that Tom's familial world was one lacking the pillared support required to provide him with a vital, secure base.

Betty, his more dependable and present parent – exposed in her family of origin to a marked lack of emotional availability – had a strikingly consistent 'absence' about her from the description presented; she happened not to be present when Tom sustained his first RTA, maintained she had no memory of the medical outcome following hospitalisation, no memory of his cycling accident at 8 years old which resulted in further medical examination, nor any memory of the head injury Tom sustained aged 14, which again resulted in hospital admission. By any objective criteria, Tom was slipping through the safeguarding/protective network of the era and familial circumstances in which he lived. Accumulative parental neglect – known to be harder to pin-point – rather than deliberately abusive parental behaviour was clearly the case here and, if professional curiosity had been sufficiently robust then this family would have been eligible for a systemic intervention through either social services, Child Guidance – the fore-runner of CAMHS – or both, from which Tom and his family stood to benefit.

No doubt as a strategy to survive in the face of domestic misery and the absence of partnership strength to support her expanding family, based upon her own experience and core belief in school as the great saviour, Betty sought to ensure Tom's wellbeing would be nurtured through academic scholarship – replicating a pattern of huge importance to her own survival. Her emotional resources so depleted, parental responsibilities multiplying, the sheer weight of awfulness yoked upon Tom's mother would certainly have been psychological factors present in the accruing powder-keg emerging within Tom's internal world. A world which, it is all too easy to forget, traumatically received three – externally verified accounts of – significant blows to the very part of his anatomy that is designed to protect our cognitive processing mechanisms. Against this canvas, it is systemically critical to add the near impossibility of imagining the aching hollowness present for an early adolescent placed on a podium – inscribed with huge socially constructed significance – as a consequence of an early display of academic promise. This is particularly poignant for a child whose sensitivity we learn of first hand, consistently worshipped his baby sister – when raging jealousy of her privileged innocence may well have been present too and without a context to explore within. Tom's childhood circumstances certainly interacted disproportionately with the three distinct domains of physical, mental and emotional health, illustrating the need to investigate all three proportionately under a single ark of concern for the learning of lessons.

Children who act on an urge to acquire things illegitimately in early adolescence quickly have this behavioural trait described as 'stealing'. Rarely is it viewed primarily as a subconscious signal that all is not well and Tom, so typically for a child not properly noticed, held close or deeply nurtured by at least one protective parent, soon became known to the equivalent of the youth justice system (labelling him unhelpfully in the process) but not to either CAMHS (for his emotional and mental health – which would probably have labelled him more usefully) or to those responsible in child paediatrics for reviewing the impact of repeated mTBI's on his development. For Tom in his mid-teens, to be clear, the only 'agencies' active in his life were his, probably embarrassed, private school – unlikely to be au fait with the youth offending service – and his struggling, exasperated, mown-down and neglectful mother. His father, Donald, might have been better able to be present for Tom if systemic family therapy had been imaginatively offered. That Tom and his family were let down very badly in the context of their lived experience was clearly the case, classically he nose-dived from the very podium that serves to launch his peers, the posh-boys whose world he had merely tasted as if tasting honey for the first time, providing momentary comfort but unsustainable and transferable to his home on the other side of the proverbial tracks.

The need to 'get-away fast' is symbolised the world over by the lure of revved-up motorised vehicles and for Tom both motorbikes and cars took his fancy. For a mid-adolescent to crash a vehicle is hardly newsworthy, but that he was involved in a series of RTAs is remarkable, since we know Tom was observed to have prowess on the sports field, which would suggest his physical co-ordination and stamina were not in question, and also we know that he had the emotional support at that time of a vicar with a shared love of motorcycling. We also know that repeated mTBI's cumulatively effect cognitive processing. This discourse was massively submerged in this case.

It is inevitably tricky to apply weight proportionately to the multiple strands that contributed to the life Tom lived. However, to me as a systemic psychotherapist with clinical experience across CAMHS, Youth Justice, social work, marital discord, substance misuse and brain injury contexts, the absence of critical systemic information until the Chair of the Serious Case Review shared her perspective meant that lots was hidden, known but not shared or systemically reviewed. In turn, Tom and his family were deprived of a vital narrative throughout his foreshortened life. Many lenses were raised in isolation and in a haphazard fashion with an absence of meta-level curiosity. Gradually there was collective heave on the part of the professional systems, framing Tom as responsible for his own downfall. It was within this fudge that buck-passing took hold and clinical responsibility leached away, the professional system, I would suggest, increasingly reflecting the dysregulated internal world of a man with multiple mTBI's.

Notes

1 As a psychologist with a specialist interest in neuropsychology, I am aware of the literature on the cumulative effects of mild TBIs (mTBIs). Yet, I remained unaware of Tom's previous injuries (except his accident in 1988) until after his death. This knowledge may have proven useful in helping to provide Tom with the support he needed. My mother, Betty, has since reflected that she did not consider these injuries to be relevant, and in fact could not recall the specific details of at least two of the incidents. Betty still feels that these events were not relevant and in fact reflected that it was family discord that led him down the path he chose.
2 It is a difficult issue to address but Betty struggles to express herself and her emotions, and always has done. She was given the opportunity to provide details of her experiences throughout this book but in many cases the

detail is lacking. Please see Professional reflection 1.2 for a more objective perspective on this.

3 The head injury was recorded in Tom's medical notes yet this may not have been fully explained to his parents, as Betty had no memory of any 'injury'.

4 This was Tom's reflection on this time when I asked him about it years later.

5 On this occasion Betty 'paid off' the person whose car had been hit in order to prevent legal involvement.

6 This information was given to me by his friend, much later in 1996, after Tom's accident. Prior to this we, as a family, were unaware it had happened.

7 It is unclear what is meant by this but it was probably the belief that he was not interested in seeking support.

Chapter 3

Reflections on a life-changing accident

Chapter 2 tells the story of Tom's life up until the beginning of 1993 when he began living at a homeless shelter. During the course of 1993 we saw very little of Tom, but he had started to make some improvements in his life; he had started to reduce his drug taking, had found himself somewhere to live and was beginning to pick up some part-time work. It would be wrong to paint a truly positive picture of that year, but it is true to say that things were better for him than they had been in the previous year. Tom also started a new relationship with a young woman named Faye. Faye was a stabilising influence in Tom's life.

My only real memory of seeing Tom that year was in December just before Christmas – 22 December 1993. It was the beginning of the school holidays and Betty and I had gone into the local town to do some Christmas shopping. While we were in town we went into a local car care shop to pick up some essentials for mum's car. While in this shop, we bumped into Tom. He had been working on a friend's car and was picking up a few bits he required before taking it out on a test run later that day.

I remember thinking that Tom was very different to the way that he had been on many of the previous occasions I had seen him. He seemed more positive and full of life. He told us about Faye and how happy he was and that he had been doing some part-time work as a mechanic, which was why he had been asked to do this work for his friend. This was around lunch time. I remember very clearly wondering whether this would mean more opportunities to spend time with him. He had been so distant in the few years since leaving home that I was keen to try and build a relationship with him. In many respects, I did in fact get what I was wishing for. This day did mark a new chapter in my relationship with my brother and an opportunity to build a closer relationship with him, but it was not in the way I would have imagined at that time.

The night of the accident

The text that follows outlines the events of that night back in December 1993 from three perspectives – mine, Tom's[1] and Betty's. I have also included Anna's perspective later in the chapter but, as she was in Germany at the time, she was not present that night.

The accident

After having picked up the pieces he required from the car shop, Tom returned to his friend's house where he set about putting the finishing touches to the car. The car belonged to his friend, but it became clear to us after the accident that the car was neither taxed nor insured. Tom was not insured to drive it.

At some point that afternoon, Tom got in the car to test drive it, with his friend in the passenger seat and his girlfriend, Faye, in the back. Eye witness testimony from the driver of the vehicle behind stated that just before approaching a small roundabout, Tom attempted to brake. The car was travelling at approximately 40 miles per hour but it did not seem to respond when the brake lights went on. The details after the accident suggested that the car's turbo jammed, but it is unclear what exactly happened. The eye witness account states that the car clipped the nearside pavement, causing it to spin round. Tom fought with the car and attempted to regain control but instead it smashed side-on into a lamp post. His friend in the passenger side had experienced minor cuts and bruises but was otherwise unscathed. Faye had been in the back of the car with no fitted seat belt. She had seen the events unfolding and had on instinct got down onto the floor of the car between the seats, which meant she also walked away with only very minor injuries.

It was Tom's side of the car that had crashed into the lamp post, causing a large indentation in the driver's door that made it impossible to get out of that side of the car, not that Tom was physically capable of doing so. The force of the impact had caused Tom's brain to reverberate in his skull. It impacted at force against the left-hand side of his skull, causing a blood clot to form. Tom was drifting in and out of consciousness and was clearly very seriously injured. The fire brigade, police and ambulance services arrived but were unable to do anything until the local electricity board had managed to make the lamp post safe. The fire brigade then cut open the roof of the car in order to get Tom out. He was then taken by ambulance to the nearby hospital. Tom had sustained severe swelling to his brain and they operated later that night to reduce the pressure. He was admitted to intensive care and placed in an induced coma.

After Christmas shopping, Betty and I returned home for tea. It was a Wednesday and my regular activity on a Wednesday evening was to go swimming at the local pool with my best friend, Grace. So, after tea, I packed my swimming stuff and off we set in the car to pick up Grace. We had got half way through the estate when I realised that I had forgotten Grace's Christmas present. Betty turned the car around and back we went to pick it up. This was around 6.30pm. When we entered our cul-de-sac we saw a police car parked outside our house. The police officer had come to tell us that Tom had been involved in a major car accident and that it was necessary to go straight to the local hospital. He was unaware of the prognosis beyond stating that it 'did not look good'. Betty did not want me to go to the hospital at that stage and instead it was considered better for me to continue with the arrangement while Betty and Eric went to the hospital. Betty was struggling to know what to do and was not really thinking straight. It was at this point that the police officer offered to take me to Grace's and then on to the swimming pool so Betty and Eric could go straight to the hospital with Faye. The plan was for them to pick me up again later.

Betty's story

Betty then left in the car with Eric and Faye (who had been driven to our house by the police officer). On arriving at the hospital they were asked to wait in the relative's room of the local accident and emergency department. Tom was in resuscitation. The doctors identified that Tom had extensive pressure building up in his skull due to the force of the reverberation damage. They knew that operating on him would be the only way to save his life. Betty then had to return to the swimming pool to pick me up and drop me home with Eric, before returning to the hospital to be with Tom. The surgery was successful but Tom was placed in an induced coma in order to allow his brain to rest as much as possible. He was taken to intensive care. Besides the brain injury, Tom had broken his shoulder and jaw on his right side.

My story

I was only 12 years old at this point in time. We picked up Grace and had got half way across the town when the police officer started asking me some questions about my brother. At first these were general questions, ones that would be expected of a person who was taking an interest in someone who had just experienced an unfortunate set of circumstances. This line of questioning then extended to more pointed questions about what Tom had been doing for a living, what car he drove and whether I knew if his car was taxed and/or insured. I had never been interrogated by the police before and, thankfully, have not been since, but I quickly realised what was happening and stopped talking. He was trying to identify whether the accident was my brother's fault. He mentioned his history of drug use and wanted to know if he had been 'high' that afternoon when we saw him. I remember being so angry. I was a 12-year-old girl who had just found out her brother was in hospital and may not make it through the night. I had been shipped off to a social event I did not wish to attend and was now being interrogated by a police officer about the character of my brother, without an adult present. On arriving at the swimming pool, the police officer dropped us off on the opposite side of the road. It was only after he had driven off that we realised the pool was, in fact, closed for Christmas. We then had to wait two hours before Betty was in a position to pick us up again.

I remember the time we spent standing outside the pool really clearly. This was in the days before mobile phones were commonplace so I used a local phone box to call a friend of mine that lived on that side of town. I also used the phone box to call the A&E department in order to pass a message to Betty to let her know where I was. I remember being angry and very upset. I kept repeating to Grace and my other friend that I was terrified he was going to die and that I would not be there to say goodbye. I remember also repeating how angry I was with Betty – I felt I had a right to be there. I felt side-lined. This was to become a regular feeling over the next few months. I don't remember much about returning home that night and have very few clear memories of many of the following days, except Christmas day.

Intensive care and high dependency

Christmas that year was just awful. Tom had only been in hospital two and a half days and we still did not know if he would make it. The staff in intensive care had not attempted to bring him round from his coma. I remember that we were going to my step sister's (Eric's daughter's) house for Christmas day. Betty said this was because we couldn't do Christmas at our house because of what had happened with Tom, but I am sure that the plan had always been to go there for Christmas day. I recall that Betty and I argued about this on Christmas morning. She viewed going there as being good for us; some normality at a time when everything was so abnormal. I did not agree. I remember very clearly wanting to do pretty much anything except go and play happy families while my brother was lying in a hospital bed, potentially never to wake up. We did go, however, and the day was subdued to say the least. I recall spending a lot of time sat in the toilet in an attempt to get away from the rest of the family – I just wanted to be alone.

Tom remained in intensive care for five weeks. He had been placed in an induced coma and the staff then struggled to get Tom to come round without injuring himself. On several occasions they attempted to wake him up but he would thrash around wildly in the bed, trying to pull out the tubes to the infusion pumps. They would then have no choice but to place him back in sedation for his own safety. During this time, the hospital staff started to make modifications to Tom's bed area in order to protect him when they tried to wake him up. They placed his bed as close to the floor as possible so that he could not roll out and do too much damage to himself. Although the bed had barriers on the sides, these were often the source of injury, with Tom lashing out and hitting himself hard on them. The nurses, therefore, scoured the children's ward and found as many cuddly toys as possible to line his bed so that when he thrashed about he did not injure himself. Tom looked a state – he was still very bruised and swollen all over from the accident, with a broken jaw that had been wired, and he lay there in a coma surrounded by cuddly toys. Tom later said he was disappointed that none of us got a photo of this as he thought it sounded very amusing. To the day he died Tom became an obsessive collector of cuddly toys, and I have always wondered whether that had anything to do with it.

Looking back I don't remember much about those early weeks and months. I don't know if that is because of time or whether I have deliberately forgotten much of it. I know it was painful and I felt way too young to be able to cope with what was happening to us. It is not for me to state here how a family should deal with such an event. Each family is different, as is each person within it. I can, however, give a perspective of a child going through this and feeling very much side-lined in the whole process. One of my strangest memories of that time was going on a skiing trip to Austria with the school. This took place just after New Year, only a couple of weeks after Tom's accident. I assume that Betty took the view that it had been paid for and it would do me good to go, to have the normality and enjoy the time with my friends. I don't remember much from that skiing trip beyond spending a lot of time lying in the bed at the youth hostel crying. My memories of this time are very disjointed and it was not until many years later that I made the connection that the reason I had been crying so much was because I was so worried about Tom.

In the five weeks that Tom was in intensive care I only recall going to visit him maybe once or twice. I think that Betty took the view that it was better to protect me from what was happening. Instead, this approach left me wondering what was being hidden from me. When I did go, it was a distressing experience – viewing a grown man lying in a bed, surrounded by toys and looking very much a shadow of his former self.

The one thing I do remember clearly from that time was the focus we all had. Firstly, we were thinking in terms of whether Tom would live or die, however, it soon became clear he would live. The focus then shifted to what kind of life he might have – will he ever wake up from his coma? Before too long it was clear he would, so the focus shifted again to whether he would ever walk, talk or write again. Overall we were just so pleased to have him back with us, and each step forward increased our sense of hope for the future.

After five weeks in intensive care, Tom was moved to a high dependency ward, a stroke ward, and then into a rehabilitation unit within the local hospital.[2] I remember that I went to visit him once in the high dependency unit. I do not recall it well but, much later, my friend Grace was also involved in a car accident and walking into the ward left me with a sick feeling from having seen Tom in there many years before.

Anna's story

During the Christmas of 1993 Anna was in Germany staying with her boyfriend of the time, before she returned to university in the New Year. Anna recalls that Betty called her to inform her that Tom had been in an accident but that it was nothing serious – he had just broken his jaw. Anna reflects that she felt she had no preparation for going to the hospital for the first time. This took place about 10 days after the accident in early January 1994. Anna recalls clearly that Tom was awake but was unable to speak. His hands and legs had been bandaged up. This had been done because Tom kept trying to pull out the infusion pump tubes and kept kicking at the rails on the side of the bed and injuring himself further (this was the first strategy they employed prior to the cuddly toys). She recalls he was hooked up to multiple monitors and infusion pumps and, to this day, she can picture the scene very clearly. She was 'gobsmacked' by what she saw. She thinks that Betty did say to her that the accident was in fact more serious than first suggested, but she certainly had not given any indication of how bad it was. She was in shock. Anna had to leave the room during the visit so that she could cry as she was so shaken by the experience. When she returned into the room she was still very distressed.

One of Anna's clearest memories from that visit is the look on Tom's face. She reflects that she did not think he knew who she was, but clearly he knew Betty. He was looking at Betty in the way a baby or toddler looks at their mum; totally helpless, confused, desperately wanting to know what was going on, why he was there and who all these people were. She said he could not articulate that but she felt that was what his expression was portraying. He seemed to want her to take away all the confusion and the pain; he was desperate for her to make it better.

The lack of preparation made the situation even more traumatic for Anna. She then had to go back to university and carry on her normal life. This was in the days before mobile phones and Anna lived in a student halls of residence so there was only a payphone available. She would call home roughly once a week for an update, but that was all she could do; there was nothing else she could do. She would come home every few weeks and visit Tom in hospital, by which point he had been transferred to the neurorehabilitation unit.

Reflections

Personal reflections

As I mentioned above, every family experience of these types of events is different. Yet, having worked with other families who have gone through similar experiences, I have noted some important patterns in the ways in which individuals respond to brain injury in these early days and weeks. I write this reflection as a psychotherapist who has worked with many families who have had loved ones experience a brain injury, but also from a personal perspective too. Through my own experiences, and that of others, I have identified four main themes that seem relevant to family members at this particular time: hope, ambiguous loss, trauma and perspective. I will attempt to summarise my thinking on these key points below.

Hope: As I recall above, one of my strongest memories from the early days after Tom's accident was that sense of hope. I use hope in a very broad sense here; as a wish for better things. One might equally call it despair, as those early hours or days of sitting by the bedside, waiting for someone to wake up, often leads to a sense of despair. This theme is more of a continuum from hope at one end and despair at the other, but I use the term hope; it is the sense of hope that they will survive, the hope that they will recover, and the hope that they will be 'ok', that drives people during these early stages. Interestingly, a reflection from a kind friend of mine who reviewed a draft of this book, was that there were signs of this hope in the story even before Tom had his accident; that his improvements just prior to his accident had already instilled in us a sense of hope, however brief that might have been.

In my experience of working with other family members, this hope is all they have to hold on to in those early days. Without this hope they have nothing; they have to hope that their loved one will pull through – it is something to hold on to when there is nothing else. Yet, I might also describe this as 'false hope'. The expectations of people in those early stages are often far from the reality of the situation they will find themselves in. Family members often talk of feeling 'left in the dark' about the likely prognosis of their loved one in the early stages after their ABI (Odumuyiwa et al., 2019; Townshend & Norman, 2018), and feeling that being better prepared for the time ahead would be helpful to them long term (Holloway et al., 2019; Odumuyiwa et al., 2019). This is a challenge for healthcare professionals who have to walk an impossible line between managing the expectations of families and ensuring that they do not paint an unfairly negative picture of the future, when the reality is that they often do not know what the prognosis will be (Lingsma, Roozenbeek, Steyerberg, Murray & Mass, 2010).

An account from a woman whose parents were involved in a car accident (a story from another survivor series book; Clark-Wilson & Holloway, 2019) highlights how she recalls praying that both her parents would survive. Having then spent a lifetime living with her father who had survived but was left with an extensive brain injury, she reflected that perhaps she had not wished for the right outcome. This is not an uncommon reflection. A family I recently worked with had a similar story to tell. The mother had been involved in a road traffic accident and the daughters reflected that looking back it may have been kinder for all concerned if their mother had died the night of the accident. This is certainly a view that I have expressed often since Tom's accident. It is one that people who have not been through such a situation often struggle to understand.

Ambiguous loss: There is a breadth of literature on ambiguous loss following brain injury. Ambiguous loss is the feeling of bereavement without the death of a person (Boss, 1999). I will refer back to ambiguous loss later in the book where it may seem more relevant, but the impact of ambiguous loss starts in those early days post-injury. Family members are in shock and are often unaware whether their loved one will live or die. This uncertainty is often difficult to reconcile. The reactions of family members are often synonymous with bereavement, but the loss is ambiguous because the person may yet survive. It is this uncertainty that makes those early days and weeks so challenging for family members.

Trauma: The nature of brain injury is different for each individual but, in many instances, the experience of the family initially after the event is one of shock and trauma. This may be because they were present when the event occurred or because it was a shock hearing the news of the event, or it may be that the sense of uncertainty leads to a trauma-like response in some individuals (Linley, 2003). Seeing a loved one incapacitated and in pain is often enough to induce a trauma response (Schmidt & Azoulay, 2012). Furthermore, hospitals are environments in which most individuals are not used to spending time. The literature on intensive care demonstrates that the act of viewing a loved one intubated and wired up to infusion pumps can be a highly distressing experience for family members (Garrouste-Orgeas et al., 2014). This is a foreign environment with disturbing sights that can often leave family members feeling decidedly traumatised. This is also an important point that I will return to, as this trauma is often left unprocessed as the aftermath of an injury means that there is little time to receive the appropriate psychological support to integrate these experiences appropriately (Schmidt & Azoulay, 2012). Again, from both my own experience and from my experience of working with others, the initial event is often quickly forgotten within the turmoil of what unfolds next. This then leaves people vulnerable to a traumatic reaction if left unresolved until much later in time.

Above, I recall the story of going on the skiing trip to Austria. While it is possible that this memory is somewhat fragmented due to time, I suspect that it is more likely fragmented due to the stressful experience I underwent at that time, and being unable to process the event as traumatic due to my young age (Ingelhard, McNally & van Schie, 2019). It is with time and years that I have been able to subsequently process it as traumatic for me. I thought very little about my experiences of that trip, beyond some of the fonder memories I had until my late teens. It was at this point that I started to remember these strong emotions of sadness and fear while I had been away, and recalled episodes of crying on my bed. It was only later still, in my early twenties, that I started to appreciate that these emotions were linked to Tom's accident and the fact that I had not been allowed the space to process my feelings about what had happened. This is probably one of the driving forces in my becoming a psychotherapist. I have since seen very similar responses in other family members who, in the same way as I did, had denied those experiences for many years. The reality is that it often takes these long years for the trauma responses[3] to be unearthed and resolved, perhaps due to a degree of dissociation from the events (Schauer & Elbert, 2015).

Perspective: Writing this book has really made me think about the perspectives of every member of my family during the events of Tom's accident, and thereafter. It also occurred to me while writing it how little I understood of the perspective of either my sister, my mother, or of Tom's. Each family member will handle the events surrounding an injury differently, and each will experience different events as a result. Betty's experiences were of seeing her son lying in a hospital bed immediately after surgery, not knowing whether he would live or die. This experience was an ongoing one for the first week following the accident, as she waited to find out if he would wake up from his coma. Betty does not share much about her emotions around this, despite some attempts to get her to express them. This may be to do with the kind of person Betty is or it may be that she struggles to express those difficult emotions. I do not know. As a mother myself, however, and having had a child who was in intensive care for a period, I can imagine that the few days and weeks initially after the accident must have seemed like a living hell. The experiences of course are different; Tom was an adult and had a car accident whereas my son had sepsis as a very young toddler. The experience of the environment and the fear that one experiences as a parent is likely to have been similar for us both though.

My sister Anna's experience was quite different again. She was unaware of the extent of Tom's accident over the Christmas period. While I can appreciate that Betty chose this course of action because she wanted to protect Anna from the emotional distress when she was in a foreign country, and probably unable to return home, I struggle to understand why she did not prepare Anna better for what she would see. Betty would argue that this was to protect Anna. Yet, it seems to me that this is Betty failing to appreciate how that would feel for Anna when she eventually did find out the seriousness of the situation. Anna was traumatised by that experience and I can appreciate why she would feel this way. She was also deprived of the opportunity to bond with us as a family over such a major event. She was left with memories of a Christmas that were 'false'. For all I would have given to have had a normal Christmas that year, my experience of it being a non-event was accurate and in keeping with reality. Anna's experience was not.

Anna's experience of being 'kept in the dark' about Tom's accident reminds me of my own experiences of feeling side-lined by Betty during those early weeks. While Betty's decision not to allow me to spend much time at the hospital was designed to protect me from the trauma, she did not appreciate that I was more than capable of inventing within my imagination scenarios and images of what was happening to Tom that were equally horrendous, if not worse, than the reality of the situation.

The point above is important. Family members make decisions in these contexts that are designed to protect others. Without open communication, however, these decisions can cause rifts and divisions within families at a time when they need to pull together. It is important that each member of a family has a choice and that there is open and clear communication about what is happening, as well as a sharing of experiences to allow all members of a family to gain a realistic perspective. On reflection, Betty's choice to leave Anna without the full knowledge of the event, and to attempt to protect me by 'carrying on as normal', did nothing but lead to greater distress for us both later down the line.[4] This is not unique to our family environment and is reflected in the experiences of other families I have worked with, and in the literature on family experiences (Clark-Wilson & Holloway, 2019).

When considering the link between Tom's head injury and his eventual suicide, it is hard to identify anything specific that happened during the period of time outlined in this chapter, that may or may not have increased his risk of suicide. This is something that will be explored further in later chapters, as clearer factors come to light that may have led to his actions in 2014. Below is another professional reflection from a hospital liaison worker (Professional reflection 2.1), whose role is to work with clients and families in hospital after injury and then after discharge.

Professional reflection 2.1: Reflections from Wendy Copeman, hospital liaison worker

As a hospital liaison worker for Headway Somerset, I regularly meet families struggling in the new knowledge of a relative with an ABI. I also meet family members at our relatives' support groups, sometimes years after the injury was sustained by their loved one. In the context of my role, Alyson has asked me to reflect on the journey of Tom and her family following his brain injury, and whether their reactions and experiences were common or unusual.

It is of course always difficult to comment on collective experience, and my work has taught me that everyone's path truly is unique. However, Alyson's own reflections, including the four themes of hope, ambiguous loss, trauma and perspective, would certainly resonate with many families I have supported, particularly looking at things through the prism of time.

Three areas of Alyson's account particularly struck a chord for me as things I have regularly observed and thought about in my work. I have sought to summarise these below:

The family's response to the injury: When I began work in this field, I quickly learnt that each member of a family experiences and responds to an ABI in their own way. This can be helpful in that family members move through the quagmire of emotions such as shock, denial, bargaining, hope, anger, grief, depression and adjustment at their own pace. Sometimes this enables them to recognise and support each other's needs, but other times their focus becomes insular. When this happens, the family stops working cohesively as a well-oiled machine and instead works as a set of discordant components, which can leave the family 'machine' vulnerable, damaged or broken.

When Alyson talks of being 'side-lined', her sense of anger and sadness at being excluded from Tom's journey is palpable. Within my work I have witnessed similar exclusions, which can lead to a sense of disconnection for the child and for painful ripples to reverberate within a family for years after the event. Parents inevitably strive to protect their children from the fear, anxiety and grief associated with what has happened. I have heard some report in the early days that their children seem little affected by the traumatic event, and so they consider keeping them away from the hospital and information the right course of action. Often, this is just a masking of emotion and not a genuine unaffectedness. Some time after the event, one parent described to me the trauma of having to decide whether to allow their child to visit their mother who was gravely ill, or whether to shield them, in the knowledge they may never see her alive again. This difficult decision had to be made when his ability to cope with his own emotions left little capacity to manage, or even notice, what was happening to other family members. Although remaining silent about the injury is temporarily protective, it soon becomes 'the elephant in the room', inhibiting children from asking questions and allowing them to invent scenarios in their heads that may be far from the truth. Conversations are effectively shut down, sometimes to be revisited at a much later time … sometimes never. As Alyson has pointed out, the effects of this can be long-lasting and devastating.

Alyson's vivid description of her anger at being expected to continue with Christmas rituals only a couple of days after Tom's accident, and her subsequent argument with Betty about this, demonstrates another common scenario – children may seem to be 'playing up' or being difficult at a time when parents, wrapped up in their own anguish, expect them to bring a mature (adult) empathy to the situation; something which may simply be beyond them. Decisions are made in haste against a backdrop of extreme emotional fragility. It is often only in retrospect that they are more carefully examined.

Support: Alyson talks about the feelings of individuals she has subsequently worked with in her professional life, of being 'left in the dark' about the prognosis of their loved one. This is not uncommon and I have witnessed family members become quite agitated about the need for this information, seeking some certainty and direction for the future at a time of utter upheaval. I often find myself explaining that healthcare professionals are not being difficult or malevolent in withholding this information, but merely that they just don't know, there being no established pattern in recovery from an ABI. In this arena, probably more than most, predictions are virtually impossible.

The lack of support available for families when someone is admitted to hospital with an ABI, as described by Alyson, is still commonly experienced, though hopefully less so where an ABI hospital liaison service is available. She talks about how truly frightening it was for the family to picture over and over the events that preceded Tom's admission. In my role, I am in the privileged position of being able to be around at this critical time, and am available to support, provide a listening ear and encouragement to stay in the moment, rather than ruminate over what has happened or speculate about what is to come.

Whilst family support post injury (and especially post discharge) per se is scant, the lack of support to children of a parent or sibling with ABI never ceases to shock me. On occasion, I have met with children and siblings living through this situation and have been able to explain the injury in a way accessible to them, encouraging questions. This has frequently resulted in tears, which have previously been held back as the child has not felt it okay to demonstrate their sadness when those around them have repressed their emotions in the way described above. Not nearly enough counselling is offered to adults living through these circumstances, yet for children it is even scarcer.

Services: Many relatives I have met have told me that although bewildering and frightening for them, the care afforded to their loved ones whilst in hospital was excellent. It is the NHS at its best. However, Alyson's account mirrors the experience of many ABI survivors and their relatives, who frequently describe a sense of abandonment once discharged. Unlike the era in which Tom was discharged, some in Somerset and other parts of the UK are lucky enough to receive an early supported discharge service (ESD), which means that for a period after leaving hospital, OT, physiotherapy, SALT and, in some instances, psychology input continue intensely at home. Others receive less intensive input from the Integrated Rehabilitation Team (IRT). When these services ultimately withdraw though, there is little else, as was the case for Tom. It is at this point that the person with the injury, and those around them, begin to see what life will be like. One of my clients who has been left with some physical disabilities post injury recently explained to me that all the time she was having rehab, there was a concentration on improvement and 'getting better'. However, when recovery dramatically slowed she remarked 'no one teaches you to be disabled'. Individuals and their families are simply left to get on with it.

Although some 20 years ago, Alyson's description of Adult Social Care (ASC) (discussed in later chapters), erroneously assessing Tom as capable of activities of daily living, remains sadly consistent with my current experience. Issues of executive dysfunction, loss of motivation, initiation and insight are frequently ignored, so that whilst the person with the ABI may be physically capable of cooking, washing and dressing, the reality of doing these tasks without prompts and reminders is much more complicated. Whilst the Care Act 2014 details aspects of need such as maintaining family or other personal relationships, maintaining a habitable home, carrying out parenting responsibilities, engaging with the community and in work, training or volunteering, measures introduced specifically to redress the service deficits experienced historically by people like Tom, these are frequently overlooked in ASC assessments.

Alyson writes candidly about Tom's other challenges with his mental health and with substance misuse. Something I often notice in my role is the ongoing failures in achieving joined-up services. Where the person with an ABI has multiple pathologies (and this is very common; for instance mental health, substance misuse, learning disability, autism and so on), either services take the view that the need for their specialism to be involved is less pressing than another, or that they don't have the expertise to deal with all aspects of the person's needs, so refuse to offer any service at all. This often means that needs are not properly considered, nor appropriate assistance offered. Despite the rhetoric, organisations working together in harmony remains rare.

Conclusion

The experience of Alyson and her family vividly demonstrates the complexity and daily struggles of managing family life and relationships in the wake of serious injury. At the bedside and whilst in shock, the decisions made by families against a backdrop of ever shifting perspective, focus and hope, may not be the best ones. Support for all family members is needed at this critical time to keep communication open and improve outcomes for all involved. Furthermore, support services that are sensitive to the hidden effects of ABI need to be available to the whole family beyond discharge, and indeed beyond NHS input. It is often when rehab progress slows that the full emotional impact strikes family members, as was the way for Tom and his family. In order to considerably reduce the high levels of relationship breakdown and development of mental health issues experienced by people with an ABI, jointly commissioned services are needed, providing a continuum of specialist support responsive to the changing needs of not only the person with the ABI, but to their relatives too.

Notes

1   It is important to note that Tom had no memory of the night of the accident so the account is based on that given by Faye, eye witness testimonies and police incident reports.
2   This unit no longer exists. It was closed some years ago due to funding cuts.
3   It is important to note that I am referring to trauma symptoms rather than any kind of diagnosis of post-traumatic stress disorder per se.
4   This is of course my reflection, as I do not know what Betty's thoughts on the subject are.

Chapter 4

Post-injury rehabilitation and discharge

Tom spent a short period of time in a stroke ward before being transferred to a rehabilitation unit on the hospital site. At that stage Tom could not walk at all and was unable to talk or feed himself. He was able to sit up and get in and out of bed but only with assistance. I remember sitting with him and feeding him a yoghurt on one of the few occasions I visited him here. He couldn't even open his mouth very wide as his jaw was still wired from the accident. I remember sitting across from him as he stared at me. I recall thinking 'does he even know who I am?' There was no sense of recognition on his face at all. He merely looked confused as if he was trying to place me or trying to make sense of what was happening to him.

In Chapter 3 I reflected on how I was experiencing trauma symptoms at that time, and that my lack of memories of the events from this period are probably linked to this response. Perhaps one of the first times I started to appreciate this was when I was about 15 years of age – about three years after the accident. Two of my friends had been involved in a major car accident and one of them, Isaac, had been very seriously injured. After a stay in intensive care and high dependency, he too was transferred to the stroke ward at our local hospital. It was at this time that his parents started to allow friends to visit. As I was the only one of our group with any experience of such injuries, I took it upon myself to visit him regularly. I remember very clearly walking into the ward for the first time. I had followed the signs along the corridors to it with no real recollection of ever having been there before. When I walked onto the ward Isaac was in a private room just to the right of the entrance, but I wasn't able to go into the room. Instead I was frozen to the spot, looking intently at a chair next to one of the beds in the open bay elsewhere on the ward. I experienced a rising sense of anxiety and, for the first time in my life, started having a panic attack. I realised in that moment that this was the bed Tom had been in and the chair I was looking at was the one he had sat in that day while I fed him his yoghurt. My reaction was short-lived and I did continue to visit Isaac on a regular basis but it was the first time that I started to appreciate the impact the accident might have had on me.

Inpatient rehabilitation

On transfer to the rehabilitation unit, Tom's recovery started in earnest. He was surrounded by nursing staff, physiotherapists, SALTs, OTs and a neuropsychologist who all worked tirelessly to bring Tom back to us. Faye and Betty visited the hospital on a daily basis throughout this period, from February 1994 to the end of June 1994 when he was discharged.

In the early stages Tom could do very little for himself. Betty and Faye would have to be there to help him shower and to take him to the toilet as he struggled with the nurses doing his personal care. Each stage of his recovery was exhausting and terrifying but filled with a real sense of hope. Every time he was able to do something new – be it eat with a spoon, walk a few steps or say a few words, we felt like he was coming back to us. We were filled with hope that he was going to be fine. None of us had any idea of what was ahead of us. The staff were great but, other than acknowledging that there were likely to be personality changes, they did little to prepare us for what Tom might be like post-injury. The team around him were great in terms of his rehabilitation and he received extensive support, however, as family members, we were somewhat on the periphery of this process.

Betty recalls that her first real experience of the changes in Tom came one afternoon when Faye had taken Tom out in his wheelchair for a few hours. The staff had given them permission to leave the rehabilitation unit but with strict instructions to stay within the hospital grounds and to return within the hour. Instead they went into town. On returning to the hospital, Betty and Eric were waiting. Eric was always a stickler for rules and regulations and could not comprehend that someone would so blatantly contravene hospital policy. He started to argue with Faye and Tom forcefully, stating all the things that could have gone wrong, that something terrible could have happened and there would have been no insurance. During his 'speech' the nurse who was present started to stiffen. Betty recalls that the change in her body language was very palpable – she was 'steeling herself for an eruption',[1] which inevitably came. The nurse knew all too well that Tom would be unable to contain his anger and aggression when challenged in this way, and she was right. It was the first clue as to what we would have to learn to live with. Prior to Tom's accident he was unlikely to have taken this kind of challenge well anyway, but instead of responding crossly he was aggressive and verbally abusive, which was not his usual behaviour.

During Tom's time in the rehabilitation unit I was allowed to visit him more often than I had previously done, but still I felt detached from the events in the hospital. It was not until Tom was discharged that I was able to start to understand for myself the full extent of his brain injury. Anna came to visit Tom every month, when she came home from university, until he was discharged. Anna recalls that she thought at the time that the accident would turn his life around. She reflects that for the first time in a very long time, Tom seemed settled and happy. He clearly loved Faye and she loved him. They were happy together.

Discharge from hospital

Tom left hospital in June 1994 and moved in with Faye in an adapted bedsit in the local town. It was his discharge from hospital that marked a rapid decline in the support that Tom received as part of his rehabilitation. Tom had little in the way of community physiotherapy, SALT or OT in those early weeks post-discharge. He had reached a point within the rehabilitation unit where he was able to walk a few steps and that seemed to be viewed as sufficient. He was still in a wheelchair most of the time and had difficulty speaking clearly.

Tom's brain injury had caused right side hemiplegia; his right arm was immobile and could only be moved by physically moving it with his left hand, and his right leg was able to tolerate some weight but he had to swing it round to walk rather than moving it under him as he did not have the ability to lift it. Due to the effort this involved he could only walk a few steps before having to return to his wheelchair. Other obvious deficits included an inability to smell food. He noticed fairly soon after discharge that he could taste types of food (bitter, sweet, salt or sour) but he had no ability to smell. This led to a limited ability to enjoy food. He also had no sense of hunger. The part of his brain that triggered hunger had been damaged in the accident. This meant he needed close care to ensure he remembered to eat – a role that Faye provided for him attentively. Although this period of time was very difficult for all of us as a family, it is fair to say that it was Faye that bore the brunt of it. She had looked after him every day while he was in hospital and she continued to do so on his discharge. Faye received no support in her new-found role as Tom's carer. The only 'support' they received was occasional visits from a named social worker.

Tom's social worker was able to provide Tom with access to a special day care centre for adults with brain injury. Here he struck up a friendship with one of the support workers who started trying to teach Tom how to do woodwork. Tom enjoyed going to the centre and he seemed to be coping extremely well despite the challenges ahead of him. Things seemed calm. It was around this time, about six months post-discharge, that Faye and Tom moved into another larger bedsit in the town that was more suited to Tom's physical disabilities.

As well as the physical impairments, there was clear evidence in those early days that Tom's cognitive and emotional abilities had changed. He was very quiet in those first several months after discharge. Looking back, I suspect that he was struggling to process most of what was going on around him. One of his biggest areas of deficit, besides memory and executive impairment, was selective attention and speed of processing. This meant that, unless he was in a quiet environment with little or no distractions, he found it difficult to follow conversations. He also took a lot longer to process information than people around him. This meant he would sit there quietly while we were talking and suddenly chip in with a comment about a topic we had been discussing some minutes before. Tom was also showing emotional difficulties; he found it hard to control his emotions and would easily become angry or distressed about seemingly irrelevant things. Tom's inability to deal with these situations often gave others the impression in those earlier days that he was more intellectually impaired than he was. In Tom's own words, people often used to assume he was 'hard of thinking'. This segregated him from society.

Life post-injury

Time seems to fly by when you are living through situations such as these. Christmas 2004 was soon upon us, and although Tom was very distressed at it being the anniversary of his accident, the rest of the family enjoyed a pleasant Christmas, pleased that we were able to spend it with him. This seemed a huge achievement given where we had been the previous year. There was also more good news to celebrate as Tom and Faye had decided to get married, with the wedding booked for

June 1995. The event was meant to be a low-key affair at a registry office, but as Faye's mum was into spiritualism, there was also going to be a 'hand-binding' ceremony in the woods near the town where we lived. June came by before we knew it. Tom and Faye's hand-binding ceremony was beautiful; the weather was fantastic and Tom looked so happy that day in his top hat and tails and big well-polished army boots; his choice of attire for all future formal events. He was even able to walk across the circle to where Faye was standing for the hand-binding itself. For a brief moment, we could all be forgiven for thinking that the worse was certainly behind us.

For Tom that was not to be the case. Only two months after his wedding, Faye left him for another man. Faye had painstakingly spent the previous few months ensuring that Tom was able to wash and dress himself unaided, could use the washing machine and could cook very basic meals for himself. She had known she was going to leave. We as a family never got a chance to talk to Faye about what happened. To this day, when Betty describes this it is clear she is still full of anger for Faye's behaviour. My feelings are more complex. I wonder why she went through with the wedding when she clearly already knew she was going to leave. I wonder what must have been going through her mind on that day when she seemed so happy. I can only imagine that she was struggling to come to terms with what she had to do.

Faye and Tom had been together for only a short time before his accident so it would be unfair to suggest that their relationship was in any way serious. It had become that way because she chose to stick by him after the injury and became his full-time carer. This is a huge undertaking for anyone, let alone a young woman in her early twenties, in a relatively new relationship and with her whole life ahead of her. We know that family discord and divorce are relatively commonplace following TBI (Burridge, Williams, Yates, Harris & Ward, 2007; Wood & Yurakul, 1997), and it would be unfair to assume that the process of caring for Tom was anything other than immensely difficult for her. I am sure that she took her responsibilities seriously, but it is unsurprising that she sought solace in the arms of another man who could provide her with a more 'normal' relationship and way of life. One of my life-long regrets is that I have never had the opportunity to tell her my feelings on it and that I, at least, do not blame her for her actions.

Despite that, the impact of Faye's departure on Tom was catastrophic. Tom was already struggling to come to terms with his injuries and to accept that he was not, and never would be, the person he once was. This sudden blow led his mental health to decline rapidly and was the catalyst for his return to substance abuse. Tom was angry, depressed and felt utterly hopeless; in his mind he had nothing to live for. As Anna reflects, he did not see the point in life anymore. I remember him sitting in his armchair crying and just repeating 'that bastard' over and over again. This was a term he would continue to use to refer to Faye for the rest of his life. Tom, naturally, could not share my understanding of Faye's behaviour.

It was Faye leaving that brought home to us the reality of the situation that Tom was in. We were left to pick up the pieces of a broken life that could not be put back together. The emotional blow of losing his wife was compounded by the lack of support that he received from services around him. According to Adult Social Care, Tom was capable of looking after himself because he could fulfil the basic tasks of daily living. Superficially, this was true but showed a considerable lack of understanding of the difficulties that he faced. Tom's inability to experience hunger alongside his lack of a sense of smell, meant that he frequently forgot to eat. While in theory he was perfectly capable of cooking for himself, he only fulfilled this basic need if he remembered, and in those early days he often did not. He overcame this problem to some extent by writing post it notes to himself all over the house with basic instructions on. These would include 'cook dinner at 6pm' or 'put on washing machine at 8am' etc. These helped Tom to remember to take care of these daily activities.

One of the biggest day-to-day challenges that Tom faced was keeping his home clean. This was not as simple as writing himself a reminder to do certain jobs. Tom had developed extensive obsessive-compulsive symptoms as a result of his neurological injury, which hindered his abilities. Tom would keep piles of scrap paper with notes on strewn around his flat. They were in no particular order but he would never let anyone move them for fear that he would be unable to remember what he had to do on any given day. Despite the fact that his appalling filing system had let him down on more than one occasion (e.g. forgetting appointments he had written down), he was unable to accept that his system was not working.

Linked with these obsessive-compulsive tendencies, Tom started to display characteristics associated with hoarding behaviour. On trips out into town he would regularly return home with items he had found lying about. These mostly consisted of lost or discarded items of clothing – lost shoes, tops and jackets. Even now it strikes me as strange that so many items of clothing are lost around a town, one would think that someone would notice losing a shoe. He would bring these items home and then be unable to part with them, as if they held some kind of sentimental value to him. On one occasion he superglued a lone stiletto to the wall above his doorway. When I asked him why he had done this he simply said 'I feel it belongs there'. When I suggested it should be thrown away as it served no useful purpose, he became agitated and said to me 'I have no purpose, are you going to throw me away?'

Tom also collected discarded cuddly toys, presumably lost from prams and pushchairs by small children. Again, there are a surprising number of these. Tom had no interest in cuddly toys prior to his injury and we often wondered whether this interest was related to vague memories of his time in intensive care, surrounded by all those cuddly toys (see Chapter 3). A friend of mine who read this book referred to this as the 'warm bath' of intensive care, where one feels secure and protected from the world. Tom was also unable to throw away many of his own used belongings. He would keep all kinds of things, including used electric tooth brush heads that he would drill holes in and then wear on a chain, either round his neck or on the back of his wheelchair. I wonder whether Tom's psychological attachment to these items was related to a sense that they were somehow unwanted and discarded in a similar way to himself and that was why he could not part with them. It is also possible that I am reading too much into it and it was merely a neuropsychological process caused by his injury. The main consequence of Tom's inability to clean, and the clutter that filled his home, was that he was often being threatened with eviction.

As well as a precarious housing situation, Tom continued to experience physiological difficulties. He was still unable to stand or walk for long and, with no community physiotherapy provided to him, he had little choice but to work on this himself. Regularly, I would go to Tom's bedsit after school and we would walk from there to the shop about a mile away. He would start by walking, using the wheelchair to balance himself. When he got too tired I would help him into his chair and push him the rest of the way. Within a couple of years he had managed to reach the shop and back without having to stop to rest. All this was achieved without outside support.

Tom also struggled with social isolation. Although he had some friends left from before his accident, these were mainly individuals who provided drugs for him or did drugs with him. His other friends had long since dispersed; unable to manage the personality changes that he had undergone. As such, I took on the role of being Tom's 'friend' as well as his sister. By this time, I was 15 and Tom was 25 years of age.

He would come out with me and my friends in order to give him something to do. This often did not end well. Tom hated being made to feel as though he was disabled; he would take exception to things such as people holding doors open for him, or offering to carry his drink. He would become aggressive easily, and my friends had no understanding of his behaviour. He was also unable to filter his sexual behaviour and would behave in an inappropriate manner with my female friends. This was not only something they did not understand but, unsurprisingly, was something that they found quite frightening. This made life very complicated for me, and increasingly I was unable to include him in certain situations. It was not until our friend Isaac had his car accident that my friends were able to make the connection that Tom's behaviour was a result of his injury. Isaac showed many of the same behaviours and, finally, it clicked for them.

Due to Tom's social isolation he inevitably crept further and further back into substance misuse as a way of managing both his emotional difficulties and his loneliness. On many occasions Tom said to me that he used drugs and alcohol to 'make his head stop'. He found it too hard to sit with the feelings he experienced around losing his old life and the sense that he had nothing left to live for.

Tom was on anti-epileptic medication which meant that drinking alcohol often resulted in him having seizures. During the first few years after Faye left, there were several occasions when Tom would drink too much, have a fall (often resulting in a further concussion injury) and, on occasions, would be admitted briefly to hospital. He would also take heroin and occasionally overdose accidentally. At no point during this time did the hospital staff notify us as family members. It was deemed unnecessary to involve us as Tom was an independent adult responsible for his own care. This would set the tone for the next 20 years of our lives.

Reflections

Personal reflections

As a researcher in the field, I have often reflected on how Tom is a 'poster boy' for all the things that we know to be problematic for survivors of brain injury on discharge from hospital. Tom failed to receive basic community service provision once he transitioned from hospital to home. For those who do not know the field, it is easy to assume that someone leaving hospital with such extensive physical disabilities would be entitled to community-based physiotherapy and OT in order to continue their rehabilitation. Tom received very little of this, something that was not unusual in the nineties (Stonnington, 1997) and is still not unusual today (Odumuyiwa et al., 2019). Therapy that is provided by specialists trained in neurorehabilitation improves multiple outcomes post-injury, including independence (Goranson, Graves, Allison & Freniere, 2003) and community reintegration (Kim & Colantonio, 2010). These are not just factors that are important to the survivor, they are important to society. If survivors can obtain integration within their community, and if possible return to work, they are much less likely to be costly to society and much more likely to be a beneficial and productive member of society (Parsonage, 2016). This primarily economic argument is not one preferred by carers and family members; quality of life is more important, but it is an argument that should resonate with politicians and public sector workers who are under increasing pressure to make cost savings in health and social care.

Tom's lack of access to community physiotherapy, OT and SALT meant that he struggled to build new social networks, leading to social isolation as outlined by previous literature (Thomas, 2011). Although Tom could care for himself in a physical sense, support from an OT may have enabled him to take more control over his life, meaning that he may not have spent his life post-injury living in precarious housing situations and under the constant threat of eviction (see Case study 4.1).

Finally, Tom did not receive any kind of neuropsychological input during this time. In many respects, this would have been the most important. Tom had a very limited understanding of his own cognitive, behavioural and emotional difficulties. Without this basic understanding and the support of somebody able to help him to employ strategies to manage these, Tom struggled with life outside of the hospital setting. So did our family. That kind of basic information and support would have been invaluable to us too, but it was not forthcoming. As a consequence of not having any of these vital elements of support, it is not surprising that Tom experienced ever increasing mental health difficulties and returned to his dependence upon substance use. As highlighted in Chapter 1, both substance misuse and mental health difficulties are commonplace following TBI (Ponsford, Whelan-Goodinson & Bahar-Fuchs, 2007). Particularly common is the story of an individual who already had mental health difficulties and/or substance use issues prior to developing a brain injury (Ponsford et al., 2007; Ponsford & Schönberger, 2010). These premorbid characteristics make people more vulnerable to head and brain injury from substance use. For these reasons too, Tom stands as a perfect example of the dangers of both TBI and also mental health and substance use in adolescence and adulthood (Ponsford & Schönberger, 2010).

Case study 4.1: 'Iris'

Iris was 53 when she was hit by a car on a night out. She experienced multiple injuries, including a TBI, and was taken to a major trauma centre for emergency treatment. Iris survived her injuries and was repatriated into her local area hospital, where she received two months of rehabilitation before being discharged home. It was advised that Iris should remain in hospital longer but she and her family believed that home was a better environment for her recovery. After six months at home Iris was managing well physically and her head injury appeared, at least to others, to be relatively minimal. It was around this time that the mood swings Iris had experienced since the accident started to become more intense and she started to show signs of both anxiety and depression.

Iris' family speculate that these symptoms were probably present earlier on but their significance was masked by the focus on her physical rehabilitation. Iris had extensive executive dysfunction, some memory problems and attention issues, as well as behavioural and emotional dysregulation. By this point her physical difficulties were largely improved. Iris' mood swings led to multiple arguments between herself and her family. Iris then started to leave the house when she was feeling low or after having an argument with her family. Sometimes she would simply disappear without a word, leaving her family to search for her. On other occasions she would write text messages to her family telling them she didn't want to live like this and that she was going to end her life. This would prompt the family to go searching for her.

The neuropsychologist that took on Iris' care felt that these suicidal ideations were linked, in part, to her poor adjustment to life post-injury but were also associated with her neurological injury, and that they may well reduce over time. In Iris' case, this was true; within three years of her injury she no longer felt the need to leave the house and threaten to harm herself. Iris does still continue to experience low mood and fluctuations in mood. She is still volatile at times but she no longer experiences suicidal ideation. This case highlights the interplay between neurological changes and emotional responses to a changed existence and trauma, which can lead to suicidal ideation and suicidality in those with a brain injury.

At the end of Chapter 3 I reflected on four themes that seem relevant to family members post-injury: hope, ambiguous loss, trauma and perspective. I will now revisit these themes again here in the context of life post-discharge for Tom and us as a family.

Hope: I described previously that families often talk about feeling 'left in the dark' about the prognosis of their family member. On discharge, this situation does not improve. The hope that is fostered within the hospital environment can rapidly turn to despair when the reality of life at home becomes apparent. There is not enough preparation from health professionals about the problems that a survivor, and their family, will face on discharge (Holloway et al., 2019). In many respects, the transition from hospital to home brings with it new waves of hope and false hope for both family members and the survivor. Transition can feel like such a positive milestone; the survivor is finally coming home. It is also the point when all support that survivors and their families have learnt to rely upon falls away. As noted above, the likelihood of having decent access to community physiotherapy, OT, SALT or psychological support within the community is relatively poor (Odumuyiwa et al., 2019). This brings with it a loss of that initial hope as it becomes clear that the survivor, who should still be in rehabilitation, is unlikely to continue to improve at such a rapid rate without this support.

Ambiguous loss: The grieving process that starts in the hospital continues in family members and the survivors on transition to home care. To those who are outside the immediate situation, the family and the survivor are 'lucky'; the person has survived and the family are able to have their loved one return home to them. For the family and the survivor, however, this is the time when the extent of the differences between the person as was and the person as is becomes apparent. There is no safety blanket of the hospital staff anymore, and no way of walking away at the end of a day. The differences in this new person have a light shone on them at a time when the family and survivors are already going through a time of tremendous change and upheaval (Townshend & Norman, 2018).

Trauma: In Chapter 3 I talked about the trauma of an event that led to an injury, along with the trauma of sitting in hospital alongside an injured loved one. One of the most difficult things to live with as a brain injury survivor's family member is that the trauma never really ends. People experience those traumatic events and the time spent in hospital, but before they have had any opportunity to process these feelings, they are thrown into a new set of traumas. These traumas are focused on daily living; ongoing and enduring day-to-day crises that have to be overcome in order to keep their loved one safe and functioning post-injury (Clark-Wilson & Holloway, 2019). I reflected in Chapter 3 that it often takes many years for these trauma responses to be unearthed and resolved. The ongoing daily 'crises' associated with caring for or living alongside a survivor of brain injury are one reason why these traumas do not get processed; there is simply not enough time to process them because day-to-day life is enough for anyone to cope with. I recall speaking to the mother of a man who had experienced a TBI. She said that it was not until two years after his accident that she found herself sat in tears about what had happened to him. This had been brought on by listening to a similar story on the radio show 'The Archers'. She had never processed what had happened to her family but simply 'got on with things' because that is what you have to do as a carer.

Perspective: Finally in Chapter 3 I introduced the importance of perspective. At the time of Tom's injury I was only able to appreciate my own perspective as a sister. Over time, through the work I do with families as a psychotherapist and through my research work, I am able to see things from multiple perspectives; those of mothers, fathers, sisters, brothers, sons and daughters. While there are often similarities, each perspective is different, partly because of the differences in those relationships, but also partly due to their own individual differences; this means that no two mothers will necessarily share the same perspective although their experiences may well be similar. This is also true of survivors themselves with no two individuals, even with the same injuries, necessarily being alike. Perhaps it is this insight from my professional work that allows me to be as forgiving as I am of the actions of Faye. Or perhaps it is merely natural empathy; that I can put myself in her shoes and see how hard the situation must have been for her. Regardless, the point remains that it is important to remember that everyone has a different perspective. Without an appreciation of the perspective of others the family unit cannot function together. It requires open communication and a willingness to view the situation from one another's perspective for a family to be able to successfully come together around a brain injury survivor. Certainly, I can see that in my own family there were many times in those early days when we did not come together, we did not share perspectives and we did not support each other in the way we should have done. This would continue to be an issue when managing Tom's eventual suicide. Below is a professional reflection from a brain injury case manager on Tom's situation (see Professional reflection 4.1).

Professional reflection 4.1: Reflections from Dr Mark Holloway, a brain injury case manager trained in social work

Tom and Alyson's experience is, of course, utterly unique. There are no two families who are the same, there are no two individuals affected by brain injury who are the same. Why, in that case, do I hear echoes in this story that resonate so clearly with my now 30 years' experience of working with people and families affected by brain injury? How come families tell professionals the same – or at least similar – stories, and yet this hard-won knowledge is not utilised to improve individual and family outcomes?

So, what are those themes? What are the repeating stories that Tom's life highlights?

Early stages and pre-discharge to the community: It does not take much imagination to consider just how traumatic and stressful a period this must be for family members. The very existence of a loved one is suddenly threatened, prognosis looks bleak and the assumptive-world is smashed. Family are thrust into an unknown land of uniformed staff, machines and professional terminology, there is, and can be, no training for this. But there is hope and all positive signs are grasped as indications that 'he is coming back to us'. Indeed, he is, but he is not the same, and so, therefore, all parties in the system are affected and changed too, although in different ways depending upon their roles, age, knowledge and responsibilities. Whilst the damage caused was sited in

Tom's brain, the impact of this reverberated painfully around the minds of all those who loved him.

Benefit of rehabilitation: Tom accessed specialist inpatient neurorehabilitation and benefitted from it. There is good evidence that this not only works but reduces longer term costs to the state (Oddy & Da Silva Ramos, 2013; Turner-Stokes, 2008).

Activities of daily living (ADL's), from washing and dressing, eating and mobilising, were focussed upon and all improved. Tom made progress and his family helped the team who were noted to work tirelessly. But, and it is a big but, these ADL goals are only the starting point, not an end point. Whilst focussing on physical goals is clearly vital, it is only one aspect of brain injury. If you re-roof your house after a damaging storm, doing only half of it is pointless.

Impact upon family, information and knowledge: Unlike bereavement, which is final and very definite, brain injury never ends and, therefore, nor does the impact upon family. The ongoing rollercoaster experience of hope, despair and joy was experienced by Alyson and her family. Grief is frozen when one's losses are not clear, there can be no closure, brain injury is an ongoing process (Boss & Carnes, 2012). The highs of a Christmas spent together and the seeming miracle of Tom walking to be with his bride on his wedding day collide jarringly with the lows of his desperate loneliness and his mental health challenges.

In this situation family are known to want and need information (Sinnakaruppan & Williams, 2001). How will life proceed? Will things be the same? What can I do to help? These are all natural questions that loving and involved family members will want answered, but instead family are often given either no information or just generic information. When people want a 'road-map' they are, at best, given generalisations about a condition that is extremely complex to understand (Jordan & Linden, 2013). The knowledge family need has to be created with them, over time, as the actual impact of the injury on that person, in that family, in that community, is experienced.

Failure to support/rehabilitate in the community and lack of focus on invisible impairments: Family unpreparedness for life post-discharge to the community is noted in the literature (Piccenna,

Lanninun, Gruen, Pattuwage & Bragge, 2016). It is when someone comes home that significant changes and losses are identified, and it is here that the family begins to learn how their relative has been affected and how this affects functioning and life for them all (Petersen & Sanders, 2015).

In order to fully benefit from rehabilitation, to be able to effectively use compensatory strategies for physical, cognitive, executive, emotional and behavioural difficulties, an individual needs to be able to internalise those strategies and use them across time and across settings. Tom was discharged without community rehabilitation. He was intrinsically not able to independently apply what he had learnt in the inpatient setting to the community setting. He needed specialist help to do so. This was a function of his condition, not a choice he or his family made.

Whilst Faye and Alyson worked with Tom to improve his functioning, this was ad-hoc, it was not informed by rehabilitation principles, it was not co-ordinated and monitored, and, very importantly, it was not able to focus upon those complex and invisible changes to cognition, to planning skills, organising ability etc. These difficulties, and how they impacted upon day-to-day life, could only truly be seen in the community, but by then the formal rehabilitation process had stopped, just precisely at the time when it was needed. Tom's life was saved but it was never made worth living, notwithstanding the efforts he and others made.

Scaffolding and support structure: Tom, his mother, his sister and his partner all demonstrated motivation and a commitment to his rehabilitation. Tom had all of the necessary ingredients for improved community functioning that he and his family could have brought to the table. The fact is that Tom had significant and hidden impairments to his cognitive and executive skills, he needed to be supported with these impairments. Faye played that unenviable role for a while, but this was not sustainable for her. When she left, she took with her the invisible scaffolding and support Tom so desperately needed to be able to function well. She was responsible for the prompts, the reminders, the keeping on track, the better decision making, the eating, the making of plans and initiation of actions, the mood management, the protection from others who did not have

Tom's interests at heart etc. Tom could wash, dress, cook and clean but could only do so effectively within this invisible support structure. The assessment of him by Adult Social Care was woeful, ill-informed and, ultimately, a proven and clear risk to his life. The assessment failed to see how he was supported to function better.

What could have been done differently? Specialist community neurorehabilitation, properly co-ordinated and integrated by a brain injury case manager, who works with the whole family over a period of time, could have supported the creation of a better quality of life for Tom and his family and could have applied knowledge about Tom's brain injury in a very individual way. They could also have provided a way of better informing and supporting the family, so they could better support Tom, and could have picked up sooner those issues and difficulties that ultimately led to the downward and inexorable spiral Tom experienced.

This sounds like an expensive set of services to provide – perhaps it is? I suspect, however, in Tom's case and in many others, it is cheaper than the alternative. When our prisons, our homelessness, mental health and drug services are being overwhelmed by individuals whose underlying problems relate to brain injury, it is nonsensical to not endeavour to address the root cause of the presenting issue (Corrigan & Deutschle, 2008; Fleminger, 2008; Oddy et al., 2012; Williams et al., 2010).

Concluding thoughts: The worst aspect for me about reading this chapter was I know what comes next and, more importantly perhaps, what comes next was, to my mind, utterly predictable. What comes next was also possible to change at the time, it was not set in stone. This story did not have to end this way, these poisoned seeds were sown at the time of discharge from rehabilitation, the crop rotted in the field for want of proper tending.

There can have been no guarantees about a much more positive outcome of course, but the situation Tom and his family were placed in set both him and them up to fail. The Serious Case Review following Tom's death identifies that very clearly, it is rightly damning about the response Tom received from health and social care services (Flynn, 2016).

So, here's to you Tom, the collector of lost shoes and lonely cuddly toys, here's to your retained sense of drive to improve your situation, here's to your sense of humour and damaged identity and here's to the (significant) challenges you posed to others. Here's also to the fact that by telling your story, your tormented and tragically difficult life story, you may change the lives of others. There are thousands of other 'Toms' out there. We can support them better but we need to understand more about the hidden aspects of brain injury and we need to apply this knowledge. To do so, we need to actually care about the person underneath that difficult behaviour and to practice in a co-ordinated and integrated way, in the communities where people live. We need to stand alongside individuals and their families and weather these grief-filled storms together; the alternative is not humane.

Note

1 Betty's own words.

Chapter 5

The long-term impact of brain injury

From 1996 onwards Tom was regularly using substances or alcohol to control his mood. Initially this started as small amounts of alcohol and smoking cannabis but, over time, he gradually started smoking opium too and, eventually, went back to heroin use. Tom had a fundamental misunderstanding of the nature of dependency in that he believed that if he were able to refrain from taking a particular substance for a period of time then this meant that he was not addicted. He would use heroin daily for many weeks and then would stop for a couple to prove to himself and others around him that he could. He did not seem to notice the changes in his mood when this occurred, even if he did not experience the infamous physical withdrawal symptoms associated with heroin 'cold turkey'.

Tom's accident changed him in several profound ways. Although he had always been quite headstrong, he had never been unusually angry or aggressive. After the accident, however, this was a central part of his character, and the drug withdrawal or using alcohol exacerbated this new side of him. He was volatile; one minute he would be happy and joking and the next angry or deeply depressed, and again these were exacerbated by his drug use and withdrawal. Despite my understanding that this was not normal nor good behaviour, one gets used to the way things are and, despite the effect it had on Tom, he did continue to function through his heroin use and regular drinking.

While Tom had no support from Adult Social Care, he did receive a small amount of funding to attend a day centre for adults with brain injuries, where he had started to become reasonably good at woodwork. Tom developed his woodwork into a hobby and started earnestly making a host of gifts for his friends and family with his new-found skill. Some of his gifts were lovely and thoughtful, such as two joined wooden hearts that he made for me and my first husband for our wedding present, or the bird table he made for mum because of her love of birds. Others were a little more obscure. I asked him once to make me a wooden planter for my front garden. What I received was a miniature picket fence with a miniature gate; a planter that was designed to look like a mini garden. Tom's comment was that 'it would stop the plants from escaping'. While Tom's life post-injury was not a happy one, he would regularly make me laugh with his off the wall, and often very black, sense of humour. For example, Tom would spend most of his time wearing a t-shirt that said 'same s**t different day' or 'I have a head injury what's your excuse?' He enjoyed going to the day centre. Whenever he talked about his work at the centre his whole manner would change; he was animated, upbeat and almost happy. This was in stark contrast to his attitude towards most other aspects of his life, and he was always looking for new projects to start.

It was at the day centre that Tom first met Jenny, his long-term partner. Jenny was older than Tom and had also been involved in a road traffic accident. She had a severe brain injury with very severe physical impairments; was wheelchair bound, had poor speech and right-side hemiplegia. Jenny was very funny and despite her injuries, including extensive cognitive damage, she was incredibly content with life. Overall, Jenny had a calming influence on Tom and the two of them soon became inseparable.

Soon after meeting Jenny, the pair started to attend the newly formed Headway Somerset day centre service. This was yet another lifeline for Tom that kept him busy and, for at least a few hours of the day, kept him clean from drugs and alcohol. His substance use was regular at this stage but relatively low day to day. His attendance at Headway proved particularly important as, in 2008, the other day centre was closed due to a lack of funding by the local council. Headway Somerset became the only lifeline for Tom and others like him.

Jenny and Tom continued to muddle through in their own fantastic way. Jenny was full of life but could be incredibly demanding, insisting that things were done in a very particular manner. She also lacked insight into other people's feelings or needs. Due to this, and Tom's temper, Jenny and Tom clashed on regular occasions. Tom would shout and swear at her and she would merely sit there and wait for him to calm down and then continue with her insistence on the way things should be done. For many, their relationship would have seemed to be doomed to failure, but it worked for them. Despite their ups and downs, they loved each other very much, and we were grateful to Jenny for giving Tom's life some kind of meaning.

During this time, life was somewhat stable. Although Tom continued to misuse substances and continued to regularly fall over or pass out, day-to-day life moved on relatively smoothly. I had moved away from the town where Tom was living in the summer of 1997. I was still in weekly contact with him over the phone and would visit regularly on every holiday from college and university. In 2004, I returned to Somerset and married my first husband.

Tom was the usher at my wedding. I remember in the lead up to the wedding worrying about whether we had done the wrong thing asking him. Tom did not always do well under pressure and I was concerned that I had asked too much of him. The other usher was my husband-to-be's brother who had extensive mental health problems and also had trouble with substance misuse. On the morning of the wedding we discovered that my partner's brother had failed to get a connecting coach from his home in Scotland and was unlikely to make it to the church on time. I was unable to contact Tom to warn him. Tom took it all in his stride – he simply did what he could and took the view that unless they were part of the wedding party they could simply sit wherever they liked. I was so impressed with his approach to it all. Tom and I had developed a strangely functional relationship despite the hardships we experienced over the years. At 12, just before his accident, I had hoped that I would finally get to know my brother. Instead he was taken away from me and replaced by a stranger that I was forced to take a degree of responsibility for, however, it brought us closer than I could have possibly imagined. He was so happy on my wedding day – because I was. Despite his general inability to think or consider others due to his neurological injuries, he cared about what happened to me and was so happy for me.

Although Tom had days when he would cope very well, overall life was tough for him. He struggled to come to terms with the accident, despite being 10 years on, and felt that he had lost the life he should have had. It was on my return to the West Country in 2004 that it became clear to me that Tom was in need of help. This was when he sought psychological help from a clinical neuropsychologist. Tom's declining mental health was picked up by his GP who made a referral for an assessment. I attended the first session between him and the neuropsychologist as Tom was aware that he may not provide all the information necessary without my support. This led to an assessment and appointment with the local hospital mental health services in 2005. In the initial session, the psychologist discussed with Tom the principles of cognitive behavioural therapy and the importance of trying to map emotions, thoughts and behaviours. We spent some time over the next two weeks trying to piece together Tom's difficulties. When we went back for the next session it became apparent that it had all been a waste of time. She told us that unless Tom was prepared to give up drinking and drugs she would be unable to provide any clinical intervention. She referred him to the local community drug service in the area and said that she would see him again once he was drug-free. Tom was willing to try to abstain from drink and drug taking, but he was unable to do this without support. He found community substance services difficult to engage with. Tom had memory problems so often failed to turn up for appointments and struggled to comply with treatment due to the nature of his cognitive impairments and mental health issues; he was unable to use distraction techniques successfully and had no other 'positive' coping mechanisms with which to substitute his substance use. Tom self-medicated because of the intense thoughts and emotions he experienced around his identity post-injury, and his sense of grief. Therefore, without someone helping him to manage these difficulties, Tom would remain unable to abstain from drugs for very long.

Another difficulty for Tom when working with community drug services was that he could, in fact, go some time without using substances. This meant that the organisation perceived him as not having such a severe addiction that required high levels of support. While his drinking and drug-taking were regular, and for him excessive, he was limited by the side effects of his medication. This meant that Tom was physically unable to drink or use as much as more able-bodied individuals before it had a severe impact on him. This was not taken into account. In reality they had no real understanding of Tom's neurological impairments and were not capable of supporting a man with such a complex dual diagnosis and a TBI. Without psychological intervention, Tom was unlikely to make any improvements. A specialist treatment service was required that took all of these factors into account (Walker, Cole, Logan & Corrigan, 2007).

As well as these regular difficulties with services, Tom's life was also punctuated by day-to-day struggles. He was still with Jenny and they were happy but, as stated above, things were also tough. In 2006 Tom moved in with Jenny. Jenny lived in a bungalow with regular support workers on hand, organised by her parents who were the deputies for her finances. Jenny's parents were understandably very unsure about her relationship with Tom. They liked Tom on a personal level but were not blind to his shortcomings and were concerned about his impact on Jenny.

The situation with Jenny's parents was always very awkward. From the moment that Tom moved in with Jenny there were several occasions when Tom would drink to excess or use drugs to the point of passing out. This often left Jenny in a situation of not having adequate care support around her, as Tom and Jenny were known to send the carers home early believing they could cope on their own. On one particular occasion I was on a conference trip to Pisa when I received a phone call from Jenny at about 11pm local time. She informed me that Tom had passed out again and he had left her on the toilet. She had no way of getting herself either back in her wheel-chair or to bed. I couldn't come to the rescue. I tried in vain to contact Betty but she was not available to answer the phone. In the end I had no choice but to suggest to Jenny that she phone her sister for assistance.

One of the managers at Headway Somerset decided to take on the somewhat unenviable role of mediator in the situation, trying to help us work together to come up with a solution that would allow Jenny and Tom to continue the relationship with minimal harm to all concerned. The mediation meetings with Headway Somerset highlighted another of the difficulties Tom faced due to his neurological impairments. As stated in the previous chapter, Tom struggled with attention and was easily fatigued. His speed of comprehension was particularly affected, especially if he was in a group of people. He would struggle to follow a conversation and it would take him some time to catch up. This led him to become very quiet in group situations, and only later would he announce that he had not understood what was said. More commonly, he would seize on a fairly innocuous comment that had been made and view this as evidence that people were 'out to get him'. He would fail to process any other parts of a conversation. For example, during one of the mediation meetings the manager of Headway Somerset made several suggestions for supporting Tom. She was obviously genuinely concerned and had the honest motive of wanting to try and straighten out a challenging situation. However, Tom's take-home message from the meeting was that 'she wants to lock me up'. This was in reference to a comment she had made about how he may end up in prison if he did not get his drug taking under control. From the moment she had made this comment he had lost the train of the conversation and fixated on that. He could not recall the helpful suggestions or the sources of support the manager had suggested.

Tom also had severe memory problems, but these were often hidden behind an ability to remember very specific detailed accounts from his life pre-injury. This often gave others the perception that his injuries were not that severe. He also had maintained residual intelligence that often served to impress those around him, adding to the narrative that he was, in fact, not that disabled. For example, one of his crowning achievements was being able to regularly complete the mathematical challenges on the TV show 'Countdown'. He boasted of the numerous times he had managed to get the answer within the time when even Carol Vorderman could not. His executive impairment was often missed because he had maintained his intellect and seemed quite capable of expressing himself. These symptoms of TBI are often described by those who are familiar with them as hidden disabilities (Odumuyiwa et al., 2019), of which Tom had many. He also had very obvious physical disabilities too. Sadly, at times I feel his movement problems and his shaking were put down to his drug taking rather than as being symptoms of his neurological damage.

Tom's disabilities were relevant not just to his day-to-day functioning but also to his welfare situation. Tom was on disability allowance and received a reasonably generous amount to allow him to live a comfortable existence. But this money was dependent upon constant reassessment of eligibility. Tom would regularly have to attend assessment meetings to demonstrate whether his brain injury had 'got better' or was still causing him difficulties. It is one of the areas that surprised me the most. Tom's medical discharge papers from 1994 had stated that they felt it 'unlikely that he will ever be capable of maintaining reasonable employment' due to the extent of his neurological damage. Yet, despite this and the breadth of hospital reports and medical notes on him, he still had to be reassessed. This came with its own problems as Tom would often forget about appointments he had, and so, from time to time I would discover that his benefits payments had been stopped and that he was living off Jenny temporarily while he waited for Headway Somerset to sort out his claim for benefits. This happened on a yearly or bi-yearly basis. This is not a situation that has improved in recent years. The assessment processes now for personal independent payments and universal credit are so poor that many individuals with brain injuries are being assessed as capable of working (Headway, 2018b). This is due to a fundamental lack of understanding by assessors of the cognitive, behavioural and emotional symptoms associated with brain injury (Headway, 2018b; Odumuyiwa et al., 2019) and, in particular, the difficulties associated with the more 'hidden' aspects of brain injury, such as executive impairment. The process of assessment is outsourced to external companies with no involvement of neuro-specific assessors.

It was during this time, in 2006, that I decided to become Tom's advocate. We put in place the paperwork to ensure that I was able to be contacted whenever he needed to have a medical appointment or was to attend a meeting or welfare assessment. I had become increasingly aware that what I saw when I looked at Tom was not necessarily what others saw. Most professionals seemed to overstate his strengths and hugely underplay his weaknesses. It was frustrating. He had extensive medical records documenting the severity of his injury and yet nobody ever seemed to question whether Tom had cognitive impairments that may impact his ability to engage with services, or whether he had the capacity to make decisions entirely for himself. Headway Somerset were great and whenever there was an important meeting to be had about aspects of his care, they made sure I was informed or present if possible. No other organisation, however, followed this procedure. Not once in the time from 2006 to 2012 did anyone even make reference to my advocacy role, let alone enact it. As a consequence of this Tom continued to miss appointments, often resulting in him being discharged from services and continuing to do things that adversely affected his health and wellbeing. I had no involvement in supporting this. As well as needing representation, Tom also struggled to put his trust in others, often assuming the worst of people without any just cause. I was the only person Tom trusted to put his needs first and it was for this reason too that we both agreed the advocacy made sense.

In 2009, the care that Jenny received externally was considerably scaled back. Tom had never liked having support workers in the house; they would clear up his things and he struggled with this in much the same way he had previously when he was living alone. This, coupled with Tom's view that he was the best person to provide care for Jenny, meant that he was responsible for most of the care, with small pockets of external support coming in daily. While this was Tom and Jenny's choice, it was not without its difficulties. As noted above, Tom was not always reliable enough to take on such responsibility for another person. Equally, he was not really physically able enough to be doing such physical care long term. Tom's right-side hemiplegia meant that he had already been warned to take care with exercise; to do some was good for him but doing too much would put a strain on his able side and potentially lead to muscular and osteo-related difficulties. I am sure that his consultants at the hospital would have deemed lifting a full-grown adult woman in and out of a wheelchair with one arm as far exceeding appropriate levels of physical exertion.

This physical balancing act was another reason why advocacy was needed. For some time Tom had been riding a bicycle again. He seemed to enjoy it and I have to admit I didn't really see the harm in it compared to a lot of the things he was doing to himself. There was then a period in 2010 when he was wearing his arm in a sling. When I asked him about it he told me that he had fallen off his bike and hurt it but it was fine – it just needed rest. It wasn't until much later that I discovered that he had in fact broken his shoulder during the fall and the doctors had told him he was not to ride a bike anymore because it was unsafe due to his physical state and the risk of concussion if he fell again. If I had known this by having been informed of the hospital visit, I could have ensured he took care of himself. As it was, I did nothing and he continued to ride his bike.

The physical strain of caring for Jenny alongside life's difficulties, and his inability to accept his life post-injury, meant that by 2012 Tom's periods of abstinence from drugs or drink were becoming few and far between. He was usually either on heroin or drinking alcohol, and he would smoke cannabis every day. As well as the ongoing psychological problems, physically he was in agony. He had started to experience intense pain in his hip and in 2011 he was diagnosed with osteoarthritis. Tom had always experienced pain since his head injury. Pain management post-injury is often overlooked in the medical literature and even more so by clinicians on the ground, but it is a common occurrence (Nampiaparampil, 2008). This pain from his injury, his spiralling physical health problems and his poor mental health meant that Tom's mood was very low. This low mood in turn exacerbated further his perception of pain, as highlighted by previous literature (Hoffman et al., 2007). Tom was placed on medication by his GP to help manage his pain. Unfortunately, his pain perception was very intense, and his years of illicit drug abuse meant he had a high tolerance for pain medication. This rendered his prescription medication effectively useless. By 2012 Tom was consuming about 10 tramadol a day as well as drinking at least a bottle of wine most days and taking heroin regularly. He still complained of unbearable pain.

Tom's pain also fed into his insomnia. Brain injuries are known to cause sleep disturbance (Orff, Ayalon & Drummond, 2009) and for Tom this led to an inability to sleep more than 4–6 hours a night. Until 2010 this did not seem to bother him. He would cope well on this level of sleep. But by 2012 his insomnia had become far worse. Tom was now sleeping 2–4 hours a night and feeling decidedly unwell as a result. It was clear Tom needed an operation to replace his hip.

It may come as a surprise to those who are unfamiliar with the processes associated with social services to know that an adult with a life-long disability does not maintain a social worker indefinitely. It certainly came as a surprise to me. While Tom was still under the remit of Adult Social Care as a gatekeeper for his service provision, he had not had an assigned social worker since about six months after he was discharged from hospital. Adult Social Care had done very little to support Tom up until this point. In fact they had been practically non-existent in our lives, except for ensuring he continued to have access to the Headway Somerset day centre. It was in 2011 that Headway Somerset started to become increasingly concerned about Tom and Jenny's situation. They informed me that on numerous occasions they had requested the appointment of a social worker for Tom and were asking them to arrange a case review to look at how he and Jenny were living. This request process was started early in 2011 and a social worker was not assigned until a year later in 2012. Even after the assignment had been made, there was no direct contact from the social worker and no case review was commissioned. This meant that Tom and Jenny were not receiving any support from Adult Social Care and Tom continued to struggle with the physical and psychological aspects of his injury and his caring role for Jenny.

In 2012 things started to unravel. On one occasion in the summer of 2012, Tom arrived at his Headway centre claiming to be suicidal. Tom often talked about wanting to end it all and would state regularly that he did not want to be here anymore. But this was different, it was a clear statement of his intent to harm himself. The manager of the centre phoned Tom's GP. The GP was not available and instead a colleague spoke with her. She told the manager that this was not their responsibility and because Tom was under the remit of Adult Social Care, it was their responsibility. So, the manager phoned Adult Social Care. The duty social worker informed her that it was not Adult Social Care's responsibility and it was, in fact, that of the GP's. So she phoned the surgery again. This time she was told that as Tom had an advocate the best course of action was to contact me and to make me responsible for Tom. This was the only time in six years that the advocacy had been noted or enacted. The manager phoned me. This was not because she wanted me to take responsibility of the situation but to inform me of what had happened. She also stated she had put in a safeguarding alert about Tom as she felt he was at risk. The alert was rejected on the grounds that it did not meet the threshold for concern. Tom did come back from this incident and carried on as he had before, but it was the first sign that things were beginning to spiral out of control for him.

Reflections

Personal reflections

Reflecting on this chapter raises several important issues for me with a more professional hat on. Many people with brain injury experience ongoing memory difficulties. This is one of the most common, and most well-known, symptoms of a head injury. Yet, it strikes me that in Tom's example, and in fact in many other people's, there is rarely an acceptance or understanding by health and social care professionals that survivors may struggle to remember appointments and important pieces of medical or assessment information. This is, of course, one of the many reasons why I chose to become Tom's advocate. Advocacy is a human right. Anyone who feels in anyway unable to represent themselves alone, or simply wants some moral support, is entitled to advocacy, a fundamental right under the 2014 Care Act. In many cases this is not available, despite the existence of local advocacy services and organisations, such as Headway, who take an active role in advocating for their clients (Parson, 2015). Furthermore, advocacy only works if the health and social care professionals on the other side of the interaction 'buy into it' in full. If they do not see its relevance, do not deem it necessary, or simply do not bother to check if advocacy is needed or would be useful, then vulnerable individuals with brain injuries, and others with mental health and substance use problems, will continue to slip through the gaps in our services (see Case study 5.1). This is a likely outcome as research has shown that many health and social care professionals have a lack of knowledge of the cognitive, particularly executive, impairments associated with brain injury that may lead to impaired decision-making (Moore et al., 2019; Odumuyiwa et al., 2019). The nature of such memory problems, and those associated with executive impairment, mean that many brain injury survivors will not remember to ask for advocacy when appointments are being made or they may not feel them necessary due to a lack of insight into their own needs and difficulties (George & Gilbert, 2018; Moore et al., 2019). In a study conducted in 2017, a small number of clients were asked about the importance of advocacy following brain injury. All the participants talked at length about the importance of advocacy and the number of times that they had been unable to access services because professionals struggled to understand their needs as a survivor. Yet, when asked if they felt they could benefit from advocacy themselves, they felt that this was not something relevant to them (Bennett, 2018).

A lack of insight is further exacerbated by high residual intelligence amongst survivors. Being able to articulate oneself clearly and intelligently, and be able to demonstrate one's intelligence, often leads to the assumption that an individual is not as 'disabled' as suggested by those around them (see Case study 5.1). The fact that intelligence does not necessarily equate to one's ability to make best-interest decisions for oneself when there is executive impairment is often beyond the level of knowledge of most health and social care professionals (George & Gilbert, 2018; Moore et al., 2019).

Case study 5.1: 'Zack'

Zack was a young child when he was involved in a major road traffic accident. Zack experienced extensive injuries as a result of his accident including emotional difficulties, mainly an inability to manage difficult or distressing emotions, responding with aggressive outbursts and high levels of depression. Zack also had extensive cognitive impairments to those areas responsible for memory, speech and executive function. These difficulties alongside poor emotional self-regulation led to behavioural issues such as verbal and, on occasion, physical aggression. In his early childhood these difficulties did not seem too profound, but there were noticeable changes from his pre-morbid behaviour. Initially after the accident Zack had some extensive physical impairments too, and required a wheelchair for mobility. Zack experienced good care in the paediatric hospital he was admitted to and received good support on leaving hospital.

His hospital team ensured that Zack's parents were well-informed about the nature of Zack's injuries and the likely impact on his long-term recovery. The team also supported the family in making contact with children's social services so that Zack would continue to receive adequate care on his discharge from hospital. Children's services were dutiful in their role, performing a full assessment on Zack and fully comprehending both his physical and cognitive needs.

Throughout his childhood, Zack was generally happy and well cared for. On reaching teenage years, Zack started to drink alcohol regularly and excessively, and started using cannabis recreationally.

At the age of 16 years, Zack transitioned from children's services to Adult Social Care. At this point he underwent a further assessment. It was deemed that Zack was not as disabled as he had previously been assessed to be and did not need the level of support currently in place for him. His support worker was removed and his entitlement was stripped back to minimal support, despite his vulnerabilities.

Within a short period of time, Zack became a safeguarding risk; he was drunk most of the time, took drugs excessively and was often spending time with dangerous individuals. Eventually this led to Zack becoming homeless. No provision was made for Zack as a vulnerable person so he ended up sleeping rough.

After Zack's housing problem was resolved, his behaviour did not improve, and he was the subject of several safeguarding alerts. Despite this, Zack was assessed and deemed to need no further community rehabilitation support.

Hope: Returning to the theme of hope is important at this later stage post-injury. Hope never entirely fades for the family members of brain injury survivors. The families I have worked with always carry with them the belief that things may one day get better. This is often tied to a desperation that if they can only find the 'magic potion' that will put everything right or, as in so many cases, get access to the right service, then maybe things will improve (Holloway et al., 2019). This is a hope my family carried for many years. Even in some of the darker moments as highlighted in the next chapter, there still remained a small glimmer of hope that things might improve. My reflection on this is that at this stage hope becomes a coping strategy. Rather than leading to possible false hope, having hope allows family members to draw the strength to continue the fight they face on a daily basis. This is also linked to the nature of brain injury. While the condition is lifelong, survivors are forever changing. This brings with it a small hope that maybe, over time, they will start to see the old person they loved emerging again. This theme of hope is intrinsically linked to both ambiguous loss and trauma.

Ambiguous loss: The sense of grieving never fully goes away. The sensation of living with someone who looks like the person you loved, but who is no longer that person, never goes away. It is exacerbated by those moments of hope, when changes in the person have become apparent and maybe even fleeting glimpses are seen of the former person. These hopes are then dashed by the return of the person who is not the old loved one but the new one. This is often associated with a sense of disappointment and then a sense of guilt for feeling that way (Clark-Wilson & Holloway, 2019; Townshend & Norman, 2018).

Trauma: Living with a brain injury survivor can be exhausting. There are days when it is a miracle that family members and carers can manage to even get out of bed. It is of no surprise for those who work with survivors and their families that the rates of depression and mental ill-health among family members is significantly higher than in the general population (Kreutzer et al., 2009). The combination of the tough nature of daily living, alongside a history of traumatic events (that are often left unprocessed), and the addition of constantly developing new traumas surrounding daily life, leads to stress, fatigue and burn-out (Griffin et al., 2017; Holloway et al., 2019; Townshend & Norman, 2018; Turner et al., 2010). In the long term, these trauma reactions can lead to a sense of numbness, high levels of dissociation and the disconnectedness of family members (Clark-Wilson & Holloway, 2019; Townshend & Norman, 2018; Griffin et al., 2017). It is not uncommon for family members to describe feeling as though they are 'going through the motions' of life rather than truly living. Recently a PhD student of mine began a study on dissociation. She found a self-report questionnaire that she wanted to use to measure it and as her supervisor I took a look. I found it frightening how high I scored on this questionnaire and, on reflection, I suspect that is linked to a lifetime of having to deal with unresolved trauma reactions, many of which were associated with my role as Tom's sister. In short, over time trauma becomes normal.

Perspective: In the case of longer-term care, my reflection is that perspective becomes lost, or at least it easily can be. The focus becomes so intently on living day-to-day life and merely 'surviving' or firefighting every crisis that it is difficult to see how far one has gone, or to see how far there is left to go. It becomes hard to not only see others' perspectives but to stay in touch with one's own – an effect exacerbated by dissociation. Below is a professional reflection from the Chief Executive of Headway Somerset the year Tom died (see Professional reflection 5.1).

Professional reflection 5.1: Reflection from Hilary Dicks, Headway Somerset's Chief Executive at the time of Tom's death

I recall exactly the details when I was informed by the manager of Headway Somerset that Tom had taken his own life and passed away. I will never forget that day and the mixed feelings of sadness and guilt that I had let him down.

I had never actually met Tom. In my first week of being appointed as Chief Executive of Headway Somerset I was advised that Tom had not arrived at the centre and was at home with his girlfriend (who was also a client), and was threatening to kill himself and his girlfriend's family. The manager and I agreed to get hold of Tom's sister (and advocate) immediately to inform her. We guessed that she would probably already know but we wanted to do all we could, and I recall that we were shocked when she was not aware of the dire state of affairs and she immediately took control of the situation.

Shortly after taking up my post as Chief Executive of Headway Somerset, we moved premises to a community centre where we shared the space with other groups of adults and children. Up to this point, we had allowed Tom to continue attending the centre, as we were his lifeline and, apart from his family, were the only constant in his life, which he relied on for structure and purpose. Often Tom would arrive under the influence of alcohol or substances and we were fortunate to have a side room where we could get him to sleep off the effects in safety. We kept spare clothing as there were instances when he lost control of his bladder.

Tom continued to attend for a very short while after we moved to the community centre, until one day when I received a phone call from the Headway Somerset centre manager advising me that Tom had arrived in an inebriated state and that the community centre manager would not allow him access, as there were other groups also there, including very small children, so the risk was too high. He also issued a ban on Tom. I remember feeling that my hands were tied and there was nothing I could do to argue in

Tom's favour. I knew that this was not an isolated case and we could not offer a guarantee that there would be no repeat at some later stage. I recall a sinking feeling at that point; I was frightened at what this exclusion would mean for Tom and a dread of what this could lead to.

I have been affected greatly by the loss of Tom and I don't think this will ever truly leave me. I recall attending Tom's funeral, listening to such poignant words spoken by Tom's sister and weeping. How could I be so moved and so sad for someone I had never met? I guess this comes from a feeling of sadness of the predictability of someone who was so badly let down by services who should have supported him and helped keep him safe, and also an element of personal feelings of guilt. Should I have made that fight to allow Tom to continue attending? Would he have conformed? Might he still be with us? My rational self knows that the answer is almost certainly 'no', but we will never truly know and, for that, I carry a feeling of guilt. My only reassurance is that Tom finally found pain-free peace.

As I read this chapter I reflect back with sadness. Sadness that Tom was so badly let down and sadness that although this should never be allowed to happen again, it most definitely has. I also have no doubt that it most probably will happen again.

In Tom's case, he and his family were let down not just by one agency but by multiple organisations. There was no joined-up working despite those of us who were totally engaged with Tom, reaching out, reporting and alerting those who could and should help.

I know of at least two other cases since Tom's case where individuals with a brain injury have been let down in a serious and fundamental way. In the first case I mention there is John. John could be almost a carbon copy of Tom, having an ABI and self-medicating with alcohol and substances to alleviate the pain of living with this debilitating condition. John is totally misunderstood by those around him and shunned by society. John, as a person, loves poetry and music and is incredibly creative and talented, but all that goes unnoticed. Instead, he is seen by those who should be helping him as an addict, a nuisance and a drain on Adult Social Care time and budgets.

Following Tom's case, in my role as Chief Executive of Headway Somerset, and following the Serious Case Review, Margaret Flynn made a recommendation that the local authority must learn from the good practices demonstrated by Headway Somerset. I was asked to run a training session for social workers of the local authority. Accordingly, I thought it would be good to share a case as parallel to Tom's as I could. I wanted to ask John and also to involve Tom's family and the manager of Headway who were all so closely involved with Tom. With much encouragement, the manager and the rehabilitation assistant who supported John encouraged him to be part of the training course and to tell people what life is really like for him, what makes him turn to substances and alcohol and why.

Like Tom, John is unpredictable and right up to the day of the training we were unsure if he would actually take part. We knew that there was every possibility that John could be of a mindset of not wanting to engage if he was having a bad day, or could be drunk or high when we picked him up for the training. Luckily this was not the case and John was not only ready but had prepared his words in the form of a rap.

The training went well and John showcased his talent whilst giving his audience a picture of his life feelings and fears. John came supported by his family who were proud of his bravery, ability and honesty. Tom's sister also bravely spoke openly, in detail, of the catalogue of failings that ultimately led to the Serious Case Review.

Headway, and especially John, were praised by the Chairman of the Safeguarding Board for the training content and the candour and bravery of our presenters. All good stuff you would think. How sad then, that on the day of training, one of the social workers in the audience chose to make himself known to John and to tell him just how disappointed he was that he was still taking drugs. This unbelievable act of thoughtlessness was crushing to John and within seconds he went straight back to feeling worthless, having no confidence and feeling that nothing had been learned. It took lots of work to build him back up. Needless to say, this incident was reported as a complaint.

Furthermore, how utterly unbelievable then that, within months of the training course, John's social worker decides that John's support from Headway Somerset should be withdrawn as he is not actually attending the centre. Despite the fact that he was sometimes unable to get out of his flat and relied totally on Headway's outreach worker and his key worker supporting him at home and over the phone. This resulted in me reporting John as a safeguarding case; it felt like Tom all over again. I remember being speechless and feeling disbelief that this was actually happening. Thankfully we were able to get John's support reinstated, although not without a fight.

I also recall another young man who suffers badly with depression and I would describe with suicidal tendencies following his brain injury; this young man can no longer drive following his brain injury and is confined to his home, which is located in a very remote setting. He is totally reliant on local authority transport to get him to the Headway weekly sessions at the local centre where he can meet and socialise with others like him, which was his lifeline. How sad then that the local authority suddenly decided that he is no longer eligible for transport and must use the bus service. No one bothered to check if there was a service running through his village, which there was not. This led to a very adverse reaction and once again another complaint. Again, we got the transport reinstated. I started this reflection by saying how sad I was, and I say again how sad I am when decisions are made, no doubt to save money, with little or no apparent thought of the catastrophic effects of such decisions. Where would these people be without the support and tenacity of family and organisations such as Headway Somerset to take up the fight?

Chapter 6

A personal account of suicide following brain injury

As outlined in the previous chapter, Tom had become very unstable mentally and was also deteriorating physically. By the time 2013 arrived, Tom was nearly permanently confined to a wheelchair and unable to walk more than a few steps without intense pain and restricted movement. In May 2013 the news came that Tom had been put on a list for hip replacement surgery and they were hoping to fast track him for the operation. This could not have come soon enough. In May, Headway Somerset had a series of open days at their centres so I went along with Tom and Jenny to join in the activities. It was clear how much pain Tom was in and he was really struggling to provide personal care to Jenny. Putting her on and taking her off the toilet was agony for him. This was also the first time in a while that I had spent most of the day with them both, and it was on this day that I started to get a real sense of how much Tom was relying on prescription pain medication, having taken at least 12 tablets in the time I was around.

The pain he was in was further exacerbated in June 2013 when he fell out of his wheelchair while trying to navigate a steep slope. He was admitted to accident and emergency with a suspected broken leg. As it turned out, he had not broken it but his leg was seriously injured. This further prevented his ability to get around. It also led to a warning from the hospital to take more care, as they would be unable to perform the hip replacement surgery if he was physically injured as it would slow down his recovery time. Tom's operation was booked for early July and Betty and I impressed upon him the importance of ensuring it took place. He promised to take better care of himself.

In July the date of the operation arrived. I was away at a conference on the day so I sent him a text message wishing him luck and asking him to let me know how it went later when he was out of surgery. I had no response. I should have followed this up at the time, but Tom was not overly reliable at responding promptly to text messages, so I didn't really assume there was anything to worry about. Later that day I sent him another message asking how he was. Again, I had no response. By the following morning I was beginning to get more concerned. I sent Tom a message asking if everything was ok and to let me know whether things were alright. Later, I checked my phone and I had a text message from him telling me the operation had not taken place and he was back at home. I would not have thought that much about this as operations are cancelled fairly regularly for plenty of reasons, but I also saw that I had a couple of missed calls from Betty. This suggested that things were not that straightforward.

When I spoke to Betty she informed me that Tom had gotten very drunk the night before going into hospital and had turned up there still intoxicated. Not surprisingly, the surgical team refused to operate on him and sent him home. It was unclear what would happen next. Tom seemed to be under the impression that they would not be booking another procedure but nobody seemed to know what was happening. I was angry. I was Tom's advocate and yet again he had been discharged from hospital without anyone talking to me about this. Neither had they passed on the information about what would happen next. After speaking to Betty I phoned Tom's GP.

This was actually the first time I had ever spoken to him directly in the seven years since I had become Tom's advocate. Despite the fact that he had not enacted the advocacy in all that time, he was actually very forthcoming. He explained to me that it was his understanding that the consultant had stated he wanted Tom to be referred to the community drug and alcohol service and, in the meantime, Tom would not be put back on the waiting list until he had managed to remain abstinent for a period of time. I asked the GP how long that time period was and he stated that nobody had set any definitive timeline.

During this conversation I was very honest with Tom's GP. I pointed out that there was very little chance of him remaining abstinent for a long period but, if we had an idea of timeframes, we may be able to get him to commit to staying clean for a short period of time – long enough for the operation. I also informed him that it was my belief that he really needed inpatient rehabilitation rather than community drug treatment, as he would need dedicated specialist support to remain abstinent. His GP agreed. He also stated that there was very little provision in Somerset and that the only likely way of getting a referral would be to get Adult Social Care to support it on the grounds that he was a vulnerable individual in need of specialist services.

The GP and I also talked about several other issues surrounding Tom's care. His GP, while lovely, was the first to admit that he knew next to nothing about brain injury or the long-term impact that was likely to have on Tom. He appreciated that with my background in psychology and my research specialism in brain injury, I was likely to have much more knowledge than him. We discussed how we might be able to support Tom's aftercare, assuming he could have the surgery, or any care he could access short term while he was waiting for the operation. The GP said he would write to Adult Social Care about a drug rehabilitation referral and whether they could support a referral for home care support, as this would require a social care assessment. The GP stated that he was prepared to try anything that I felt might be useful and was prepared to trust my judgement. This was a refreshing change from previous interactions with Adult Social Care that had been prohibitive and resistant to helping us or Tom.

One of the most difficult aspects of what had happened regarding the surgery was the assumption that Tom was a fully capable adult who made his own choices. He had been deemed to have made a 'lifestyle choice' so the hospital were not prepared to support him. From my own understanding of the mental capacity legislation, I was quite surprised that nobody seemed to be raising the issue of capacity in Tom's case. My understanding was that mental capacity was something that was difficult to challenge in terms of day-to-day lifestyle choices, but issues around capacity were more likely to be raised when someone's medical treatment was potentially at risk. In this instance Tom's care was not just jeopardized, it had been permanently withdrawn and nobody felt that it was necessary to ascertain whether he had the capacity to make best interest decisions for himself surrounding his own healthcare needs.

Tom was a real contradiction. At times he could be incredibly funny and at others he would be very angry or depressed. He spent most of his life living in his own little world, oblivious or uninterested in other people or their lives. But just occasionally he would show a streak of real sensitivity underneath it all. After I had spoken with the GP I relayed my findings to Betty, who was very concerned that Tom was going to be angry about me interfering in his business. It was true that Tom could be volatile at times and certainly did not like people telling him what to do. So later that day I phoned him to tell him what I had done. Far from being angry Tom actually was very glad that I had tried to deal with it for him. In an unusual moment of gratitude he said to me 'Aly, I could never be angry at you, you don't interfere in my life, you only ever try to help me. I will go along with anything you think is best, as you are the wisest person I know'. He, of course, did not actually go on to do what I asked of him, but the sentiment was there.

Over the next couple of months we waited to hear what might happen about getting some support for Tom. The reality was that nothing was forthcoming. We were receiving regular reports from Jenny, and from Tom, of drug taking at the property and some email contacts from Jenny's family informing us of similar activity. Tom had some local drug dealers and users regularly attending the property. On one occasion towards the end of August, I went to visit him and one of their cats had gone missing. I spent some time outside calling to it before considering that maybe it might be upstairs in the house. Tom had a small bedroom on the top floor, in the eves of the bungalow. There was little else up there except a loft space that the cat had escaped into on previous occasions. I went up there to find the cat hiding in the rafters as predicted. It was an opportunity to have a look at Tom's room, a place I rarely went in. His room was littered with clothes and rubbish all over the floor. It was so bad that it was impossible to find a path across the room without standing on things. More worrying was the occasional needle that could be seen lying amongst the mess. I went downstairs and told Tom the importance of clearing up the needles in future. He had always been proud that despite his heroin use, he had never got into injecting. He promised me he was still avoiding it but that some of his mates had left the needles behind. We disposed of them appropriately and I made sure he had a sharps box for future needle disposal.

It was after this incident that I had another conversation with Tom's GP. I told him that my feeling was that his mental health was deteriorating and a referral to community mental health services was required. He then followed this up later in the month to inform me that Adult Social Care had refused to support a referral to drug rehabilitation and did not deem that his situation had changed sufficiently to require a reassessment of his care needs. He also told me that community mental health had advised him that Tom was not under their remit because he needed specialist service provision. There was some positive news though. Tom did now have a named social worker who was in contact with both Headway Somerset and the GP surgery. The GP agreed to make a referral to a clinical neuropsychologist for specialist support on my suggestion, and also agreed with my suggestion to refer Tom to the pain management service. This was an attempt to provide Tom with some non-drug based techniques for controlling the pain he was in to help him reduce his drug and alcohol intake. Also, Headway Somerset had managed to find a support worker from their outreach programme to attend the appointments Tom had to go to with the community drug and alcohol service. This was an important step forward as it meant that someone from Headway should always be informed of the appointments by the organisation and the support worker would ensure Tom made it.

He needed these appointments with the drug and alcohol team predominantly for repeated drug testing to show he was trying to get clean. Their role in his rehabilitation was limited. They did not know how to manage his cognitive difficulties and did not understand his executive problems. They also decided that his level of drug and alcohol use was not sufficient for him to be a high-risk case. Even though Tom could no longer go a single day without drinking alcohol or smoking heroin, the fact he could switch between the two and not take both daily meant that he was perceived as not being an 'addict'. I did not agree. It was also viewed that his usage was within lower limits than some of their other clients, so he was deemed to be at lower risk. This did not take into account his brain injury, and particularly his epilepsy. These conditions meant that Tom could not consume the quantity that others may without passing out. This did not make him low risk. In fact, it made him a higher risk as he was more likely to injure himself when intoxicated. Also, we were soon to find that the organisation did not always share information with Headway as asked and so some appointments were missed, leading to threats of discharge from the service.

Over the course of September and October 2013 there were further problems in the house. The first consisted of some of Tom's drugged up 'mates' spraying graffiti all over the wall of Jenny's bedroom. The second was some of these 'mates' disconnected Jenny's piper alarm system and threatened her for money. Finally, Tom got so drunk one night that he ended up outside in the street shouting and swearing about how bad his life was and then had passed out in his wheelchair directly in front of the door. Jenny was unable to wake him to get him to move. Jenny phoned her sister whose husband decided to go and get Jenny and take her away from the house, but they did not want to deal with Tom as things had never been good between him and Jenny's sister. The family contacted Betty who contacted me. This had become the new norm. As I had a very young child of only a year old, I had taken a less active role in dealing with these regular issues directly but it still usually landed on me to pick up the pieces. My new partner and I agreed that as he was stronger it would be best if he went to the house, as he would be in a better position to physically move Tom if necessary. Thankfully, on his arrival, it turned out Tom was in his electric wheelchair, so my partner was able to carefully manoeuvre him inside the house and park him up in a corner before helping Jenny to pack her things. This was the final straw for Jenny's family who called a meeting of the two families with Jenny and Tom's social workers. They also gave Tom one week to get out of Jenny's house.

I was not present at the meeting that took place – I was working so Betty went to represent Tom instead. The outcome of the meeting was that the social workers felt that as Tom and Jenny wanted to be in a relationship together and they were consenting adults, they had every right to continue in this relationship. Jenny's family raised the issue of safeguarding surrounding Tom's behaviour and the impact it was having on Jenny. They dismissed this as not requiring safeguarding measures and that it was their freedom of choice that should be the main focus. Jenny's family then stated that they had no choice but to ask Tom to leave the property. Betty asked Tom's social worker what support could be given to Tom to help him with new housing and she stated nothing would be forthcoming because he was not entitled to any support and, as he was not in need of supported housing, they could not intervene. Following the meeting we managed to persuade Jenny's family to let Tom have a month's notice, but this was the best that we could do. So, by November Tom would need to be out of the house permanently. Meanwhile it was decided that Jenny would have respite care at the nearby residential unit in order to keep her safe from Tom's spiralling behaviour. None of this was suggested or supported by Adult Social Care.

Later that month Tom finally received a letter inviting him to an appointment with the pain management team in early December. It was a tiny ray of hope amid an otherwise bleak picture. The GP also confirmed that he was still exploring the neuropsychology referral and hoped he would be able to get something in place. But it felt like time was running out. Although Tom was getting increasingly unwell, I had at last developed a good working relationship with his GP, but we both knew this was going to come to an end when Tom was evicted from the property unless he could find accommodation within the catchment area of the surgery. Things were feeling very fraught. Betty and I continued to send emails to Tom's social worker in an attempt to get her to do an assessment with him and also to try and get some housing support for him.

Later in the month, things took yet another drastic turn. I discovered that Tom had gotten drunk yet again at the property on his own and had been sat outside the house in his wheelchair shouting and swearing. He had been loudly threatening to kill Jenny's family and then kill himself. Not surprisingly, Jenny's neighbours had called the care company and the police. The police had allegedly turned up expecting a serious incident. Thankfully, when they realised that Tom was in no fit state physically to carry out his threat and that nobody except himself was in immediate danger, they helped to calm him and took him into the house. They were to make the second safeguarding alert about Tom.

I was told that Tom had sat and spoken with the police for some time and had admitted to them that he was suicidal and that he desperately wanted to be clean from drugs so that he could get his life back together. He said he honestly did not think he was going to be able to do it without going into a unit. He was also convinced he would do something to himself if he was not sectioned. The police went with him to the hospital where Tom presented to the mental health team and stated he wanted to be admitted. They gently directed him back home and informed him that they would send a team out from community mental health the next day. I was stunned. Things had been rough for years and receiving phone calls late at night, or even in the middle of the night, was not uncommon. But since July things had gone horribly wrong. This was now becoming a weekly, sometimes daily, occurrence. The next morning I informed Betty of what had happened and she agreed she would go to the house to be there for the meeting. I stayed with my son, but I wish in hindsight that I had gone. I may have had a better chance of fighting his corner than my mother.

When I later discovered what happened at the meeting with community mental health, I could not quite believe what I was hearing. Apparently they had assessed Tom and decided that he did not meet the criteria for their service. I assumed initially that this was due to him needing specialist care, as previously indicated. In fact, it was because Tom was assessed as not being mentally ill. He was merely 'responding to life events'. They also stated he was not suicidal and, therefore, did not require inpatient treatment. Nor was he eligible for support from the crisis service because he was not mentally ill. I was incredulous. Given the vast literature surrounding the link between TBI and mental health conditions (Bessell, Watkins & Williams, 2008; Bombardier et al., 2010; Koponen et al., 2002), the poorer prognosis when associated with substance abuse (Graham & Cardon,

2008), and the increased rate of suicidal ideation and suicide risk (Bahraini et al., 2013; Felde, Westermeyer & Thuras, 2006; Mackelprang, Harpin, Grubenhoff & Rivara, 2014), it seemed quite unbelievable to me that this was the response. I questioned Betty and the thing that seemed most concerning was that it was unclear whether they had taken into account Tom's neurological difficulties at all. Betty's account seemed to suggest that they had put his physical symptoms down to his substance use.

Despite my absence at this meeting I was seeing Tom regularly at this point, trying to keep him positive and trying to get him to focus on the things that had to be done to pull his life back on track. I turned up on the Monday night following the assessment to find him sat in the hall of Jenny's house, which was now practically empty (the family were clearing the property ready for a complete re-fit on Tom's departure). He looked lost; sat in his wheelchair, alone in an empty house. He was in such torment that it was visible on his face. I sat beside him on the floor and asked him if he could describe what was going through his head. He said he had had enough. He told me that life was one long endless struggle for him and he was tired of fighting. He wanted to 'get off the merry-go-round'. He told me that he had decided that everyone would be a lot better off without him, and he could not see the point in his life at all. He said that he was angry at himself because he did not even have the 'guts' to end it. I gently asked if he meant suicide. He said 'yeah, I want to hang myself and make it all stop'. He then went on to say that he was too physically weak now because of his hip, that he was worried that if he tried he would not have the strength to end things, or worse still he would manage an unsuccessful attempt and leave himself in a worse state than he was now, or even as a 'vegetable'. I did not know what to say. The awful thing was that the main reason for this was because I agreed with him. I could see how little meaning and purpose his life had and I could not see any positive resolution to it. I was struggling to provide positive reassurance to him because I could not provide it to myself. I felt we were repeatedly banging our heads against a brick wall.

I was also scared. I was scared for him and what the future held, but I was also scared for me. I did not know that I would cope if Tom chose to take his own life. I had been through many things in my life but that felt like a step too far. I did not trust myself to manage. It was, in part, out of selfishness that I managed to pull myself together and find the words to talk Tom back from where he was. I told him that I loved him and I begged him not to hurt himself because I needed him to stay in my life. I reminded him of all the things we were trying to get done with the GP and how with some effort we could turn things around. He agreed and promised that he would not do anything to himself, but it was clear that was mainly because he did not believe he would be able to physically do it anyway.

After leaving the property I phoned Jenny's care manager. Tom had told me that he had spoken to him earlier that day and I wanted his perspective on what he said. The manager reassured me that he did not feel that Tom was genuinely at risk of harming himself but he promised he would keep an eye on him.

The next day I called Tom's social worker and informed her of the events of the weekend. She stated that there was nothing really that she could do as this was mental health not social care. I was furious. She was his designated social worker and yet she was not doing a thing to try and facilitate his access to any kind of service. She also told me, yet again, that they would be unable to offer up support with his housing situation. I sent her an email later that day outlining how unhappy I was and informing her that there would be a complaint letter arriving shortly. It was also this week that Tom's referral to the pain management clinic came through. This would normally have been good news but things were so chaotic Tom was in no mood to engage with it as he was, unsurprisingly, focused on his imminent eviction. Tom never made it to the appointment and was then discharged from the service.

On the day that Tom's notice expired, Betty, along with Jenny's care manager took Tom to the local housing office to present him as homeless as we had been instructed to do. In the eyes of the organisations working with Tom he had made himself 'intentionally homeless'. This basically means that he was not entitled to fast-track services as he might have been if his situation was deemed to be unintentional. There seemed to be little appreciation of Tom's TBI or his mental health problems. It seemed to me that most of the time the professionals he interacted with simply saw him as an addict and that coloured their view of him to the extent that they were unwilling to provide him with the support he so desperately needed. Without the intervention of Adult Social Care to state that Tom was a vulnerable adult, he was treated as though he was any other man in his forties who had made himself homeless. The risk his brain injury posed to him as a homeless person, or the issues that might mean he was not capable of making best interest decisions for himself, were not considered. Tom had joined the already high rates of homeless people who have experienced TBIs prior to homelessness (Bousman et al., 2010; Hwang et al., 2008; Oddy et al., 2012).

The housing department were able to offer him temporary accommodation in a local hotel and Betty went with him to book him in. Within minutes of having done so, Tom had a grand mal seizure. He rarely had seizures of this magnitude, but on this occasion it was serious enough to warrant an ambulance being called. Betty went with Tom to the local hospital and spent several hours there with him while he underwent various checks and tests. Meanwhile, the housing officer contacted Betty to inform her that the hotel was the only accommodation available and that the manager now refused to take Tom back again because he posed too much of a medical liability, especially over a weekend when there would be less support available. This meant that when Tom was discharged from hospital, he would have nowhere to go. Betty phoned me and told me what was going on. She said that she had little choice but to take him home with her but she was reluctant to do so because she did not want the housing department to think this meant he did not need rehousing. Tom was discharged from hospital in the early hours of the Saturday morning with nowhere to go except Betty's house.

Betty was 69 years old by this stage and was due to be moving in to a new house with myself and my partner to make life easier for her physically. This meant she was not capable of taking on such a responsibility. While Betty and Tom got on fine day to day, there was also ongoing strain in their relationship brought about by the events that had happened in our childhood (see Chapter 2). This meant that psychologically this was not the best place for Tom. The only advantage it served was that Betty lived in a neighbouring town, so Tom was unable to access the people who would normally supply him with drugs.

Tom stayed with Betty for the next two weeks. During this time she took him to his weekly Headway sessions and tried to progressively reduce the level of alcohol he was drinking. Meanwhile, the housing office tried to sort out new temporary accommodation. Despite our frustrations with the process of trying to get Tom access to housing, it is important to note that the housing officer did understand, on some level at least, that Tom was vulnerable. She tried her best to get him housing and, where possible, move him up the list. She was also very good at keeping myself and Betty involved in the process. This was a refreshing change given the lack of correspondence we had received from organisations previously.

After two weeks with Betty, the housing office managed to get Tom access to a bed and breakfast back in the town where he previously lived. This was far from a step forward for Tom. Back in the town where his mates were he started to invite his 'best friend' and drug dealer over. This was against the rules and he was warned on the three occasions that he would be asked to leave if it continued. I received a phone call from the housing officer about a week after he moved there letting me know what was happening. She really wanted to help Tom but she was restricted by the rules that had been imposed, so the only thing she could do was prepare me for the possibility that the situation was about to go wrong again. Only 10 days into his stay, in the first week of December, Tom was made homeless again – this time by being evicted from the bed and breakfast.

On the Monday of the eviction, I received a phone call from the housing officer asking if Tom had informed us of what had happened. I confirmed that he had not and thanked her for getting in touch. She said that they needed him to come back to the housing office and report to them so they could start the process of finding somewhere else for him to live. I tried to get hold of Tom on the phone but he did not respond. I sent him a message telling him he was needed at the housing office. I was at work and had no way of getting there but Betty had agreed to go in and meet him if he wished. He never contacted her. He did arrive at the housing office where they told him that there was no emergency accommodation available that day. The housing officer was kind enough to phone me again to tell me he had arrived and to inform me that they were out of suggestions for the time being. She told me that they had a place on the ground floor of the homeless shelter that would soon become available but that, until then, she was not sure they would be able to find him accommodation. Betty and I were due to move in together on the Friday so there was little option for him staying with either of us that week. I decided that the best option was to book him into a hotel outside of town until we could get him into the shelter. The hotel I had in mind was near both myself and Betty but was outside of the town where Tom had been living. It was also in the middle of nowhere, so limited the likelihood of him getting access to drugs or his friends. All I needed was to get hold of Tom to fill him in on the new plan. But he did not answer his phone. By the time I left work at 6pm that night, I still had not heard from him. I had left lots of messages on his phone but he did not respond – not even a text message to let me know he was ok. I was frantic.

I arrived back home at about 8.30pm that evening and tried to phone Tom again. I also phoned Betty who had not heard from him either. Eventually, by bedtime, he still had not responded, so I sent him a last message telling him just to send me a message to let me know he was ok. I hardly slept that night. I remember lying there restless, assuming the worst. I honestly thought that he had finally given up and was probably lying dead somewhere having overdosed deliberately. I was broken. I remember some years before a cat of mine had gone missing. During the time before I discovered that the cat was in fact dead, I was desperate. I remember thinking at the time that the cat being dead would be terribly sad but it was the not knowing that was really going to hurt me. I was terrified back then that I would never know what happened to it. When I found the body I had closure despite the sadness of losing him. I am, of course, not equating Tom's disappearance to that of a cat, but I had the same fear – I might not ever know what had happened to him. In many respects this uncertainty was more unbearable than the thought that he may be dead.

By the next morning Tom still had not replied and I left for work very distressed. Mid-morning arrived and still I had heard nothing. It was at this point that I remembered that it was Tuesday; the day that Tom attended Headway. It occurred to me that even with his life falling down around his ears, if Tom was still alive, he would probably attend Headway. He was a creature of habit; continuity and structure were very important to him post-injury. I phoned Headway and they confirmed he had just arrived but they were very worried about the physical and mental state that he was in. I informed them of the previous day's events and told them I needed to speak with him urgently. When he got on the phone I was not sure whether to tell him how much I loved him or to scream at him for how terrified he had made me feel. I instead stuck to the facts. I said I knew what had happened and asked him why he had not responded to me. He told me his phone was not charged and so he had not received any of my messages. I asked him where he had gone after the housing office. He informed me that he had ended up sleeping rough in a sports shed at a neighbouring school. This was not what I needed to hear. I was relieved he was still alive but, despite the views of the professionals, I felt he was way too vulnerable to be street homeless. I informed him of my hotel plan and told him that I would get hold of the hotel and arrange the booking and then phone back to confirm with him.

After having organised the accommodation with the hotel and contacting Tom to inform him of the situation, I arranged with Headway for Tom's regular taxi driver to pick him up from there and take him straight to the hotel. I was terrified that Tom would disappear again so I wanted to make sure he had no opportunity to slip away. The day centre finished at around 3pm that day and by 6pm I still had not heard from Tom to confirm that he had arrived safe at the hotel. The stress started all over again – where was he now? I knew his phone was working again as he had sent me a message earlier confirming that it was now charged, yet he was not answering again. So I phoned the hotel. Despite the fact that I was paying for the hotel room and it was booked in my name, with Tom's as the resident name, the hotel reception would not give me any information. They would not even confirm whether he had checked in. It was not until 8pm that night that he finally sent a text saying he was there and had fallen asleep on arrival. He was safe for now. Tom stayed in the hotel for another few days until he was rehoused to the homeless shelter at the end of the week.

I remember speaking to Betty on the phone after I had spoken with the housing officer. She was so happy that Tom was going to the shelter. I remember her saying that maybe this was the turning point he needed to get things back on track, but I was not so sure. The homeless shelter was very close to several outlets that sold alcohol 24 hours a day. It was also full of people with current or recovering drug problems. To me, this simply meant that he would have even more opportunities to indulge his substance misuse and potentially fall even further into despair. He was also vulnerable. I was firmly of the opinion that he had lost any capacity to make informed choices about the people he was spending time with and who he should trust. This would make him very prone to abuse, along with his physical disabilities that meant people would be better able to take advantage of him.

The reality was there was nowhere else for him to go. We were now moving in with Betty and had an 18-month-old son who we did not want to be exposed to Tom's lifestyle. Housing him with us was not possible and we could not afford a hotel long term until something permanent became available. The only hope left was that we could convince Adult Social Care of his need for supported housing so he could be moved quickly. I did not hold out much hope of this. Tom's social worker had started to look in to the possibility of supported housing for him but every time we followed this up it felt like nothing had been done. Yet we kept trying. The email and phone correspondence between Betty and I and Adult Social Care was weekly, sometimes daily, with no real outcome. Other problems also followed in that the referral Tom's old GP had made to neuropsychology was cancelled on the grounds that he had no forwarding address and, until he had a GP, we were unable to get a re-referral to the pain management team.

In January of 2014, Tom was admitted to hospital following a heavy drinking session. It was at this time that he asked for a referral back to community mental health on the grounds that he was depressed and suicidal. The mental health team did not contact him. They did not even do a re-assessment. It was deemed that things had not changed since Tom's last assessment in early November so there was no need to follow it up. This was despite two further safeguarding alerts having been raised about Tom during this period. This should have been evidence of a situation that was out of control and of a person who was unwell. It was also during this first month in the homeless shelter that Tom lost his mobile phone for the first time. He told us he had lost it but it soon become apparent that it had been stolen.

On a more positive note, the GP responsible for the homeless shelter was active at trying to help tackle Tom's pain management issue. While there was no referral back to pain management, the GP did instigate the use of medication patches that would offer a slow release throughout the day. The GP was also aware of Tom's dependency issue and started the dosage high and was gradually trying to reduce the amount to reduce his tolerance to the drug.

Throughout January and February 2014 I saw Tom on several occasions. Tom was no longer eligible for transport to take him to Headway, which meant that Betty had to take him and I would fill in on the occasional day where I did not need to be in work. We also went for coffee regularly. He was never the cleanest or most well-presented individual, but his self-neglect was becoming difficult to ignore. He looked dishevelled and unwashed most of the time. It was also evident that his drug and alcohol addictions were spiralling even further out of control. Tom had always prided himself on never using needles to take heroin, but in these final months he was injecting fairly regularly and half the time didn't even really know what time of day it was. He was also constantly being threatened with eviction from the homeless shelter because he continued to take drugs and drink alcohol on the premises.

When I saw him for my birthday in February he finally admitted to me that he had now lost three phones to theft. I was already suspicious this was the case. I had tried to phone him one morning to see how he was and the person who answered the phone was not Tom. They asked who I was and when I told them and asked who they were, the phone went dead and was switched off. I guessed it had been taken but it was not until the next phone went missing too that Tom finally admitted what was happening. During the final six months of his life, Tom was constantly reporting to us incidents of people stealing his money or phones. There had been a time when we did not go more than 48 hours without exchanging texts, but during these final months I got used to not hearing from him for days, sometimes weeks, at a time. This was usually because his phone had been stolen and he would then have to get a replacement number. It would be ages until I would find out and make sure he had my number again.

By his birthday in March it was clear that things were bleak. Tom was not sleeping and although his pain seemed more under control, this was clearly as much to do with his substance misuse as it was to do with any of the efforts of the GP. Tom had made a lot of new 'friends' in the local area. Anna was told by some friends of hers who worked in the area that the people Tom was spending time with were known drug addicts and prolific shoplifters, and were often arrested for disorderly behaviour. We alerted housing and Adult Social Care but unless they chose to act there was nothing we could do but sit back and watch the events unfold.

In April 2014, Tom was finally found permanent accommodation in a council-owned bedsit. Although it was a relief that Tom was no longer living precariously under the constant threat of eviction, our fears about the abuse he was experiencing from those around him, and his increasing self-neglect, were not allayed. Tom was not in a supported housing initiative so we were the only ones looking out for him. He had also been housed in the worst part of town, where the likelihood of abuse was just as high as in the homeless shelter. The housing officer was not blind to our concerns and we were grateful to her that she contacted the police who had a community hub almost directly opposite Tom's flat. She gave them some background about Tom's situation so the police were looking out for Tom too.

It was at this time that Tom encountered yet another setback. I received a phone call from the manager of Headway informing me that Tom had turned up drunk to the centre, had been verbally abusive to another client and to someone else in the community centre where the centre was housed. Turning up drunk and passing out was fairly common. Despite it being against Headway's policy to accept clients who were under the influence of drugs and alcohol, they had for many months (in fact years) turned a blind eye to Tom's behaviour because they knew he desperately needed support. Unfortunately, the abusive behaviour on the grounds of a community centre, had been a step too far. The manager was phoning to inform me that she was going to have to discontinue Tom's access to Headway. Headway were also struggling to continue to provide a support worker for Tom's drug rehabilitation appointments. On numerous occasions the support worker had turned up to find Tom so intoxicated that he did not even know who he was. The support worker had been compromised too much by this, so the care was withdrawn. It is probably testament to how bad things were at this time that I remember simply laughing, as well as reassuring the manager that I did not in any way blame her for the decision that had been reached. The idea of someone with a brain injury being so unruly that they got thrown out of Headway amused me. It did not of course amuse me at all, but we had been living this for such a long time that laughing at the ridiculousness of it all was about all I had left.

Meanwhile, back at Tom's flat, things were not going well. All of Tom's 'friends' that he made over the years and, most importantly, some of the particularly undesirable characters who had befriended him at the homeless shelter, all flocked round to his flat. It was clear that they were dealing out of the property and many of them were 'living' there permanently or otherwise. The police kept a close eye on the situation and tried to intervene as much as they could. During this time he also failed to attend many appointments with his GP and with the drug and alcohol service. Any hope that Tom would be able to get 'clean' and get the hip operation he was in urgent need of had disappeared months before. We were now left asking the question – what happens if his hip gives out? This was a question nobody seemed to be able to answer for us.

During this time Betty and I saw Tom reasonably regularly, but we were never invited to his flat. He always arranged to meet us at the coffee shop we enjoyed in town. In hindsight this was probably so that we would not see the state that the property had got in, or so that we did not have to risk bumping into the other people at the property. The police tried to get Tom involved with the 'Link' project on the estate designed to improve the area, with a view to making new, more suitable friends for him.

On the 18th June I saw my brother alive for the last time. I had gone into town when I saw Tom in his wheelchair ahead of me in the street. To this day I will never be able to forget the thoughts that went through my head. I am ashamed to admit that when I saw him my heart sank. I had reached a point where I was so tired of the constant battling and things felt so pointless. I had come into town to do something nice for myself and I did not want it ruined by listening to the latest bad news that had befallen him. I started to walk slower. I remember thinking that if I just let him go by as if I had not seen him then I would not have to deal with it. I can only now hold on to the fact that the guilt I felt at these thoughts was enough to make me approach him and ask how he was.

Tom was very distressed. He told me that money had gone missing from his flat and that his bank card had gone. He admitted that one of the people he had allowed to stay at the flat had asked to borrow money the week before and he had given them his cash card and pin number to take some money out for themselves. They had now stolen the card and his money and with the card would be able to empty out his bank account. Tom was in town to go to the bank to stop his card and to ask for an overdraft facility to keep him going until his next benefit payment 12 days later. I was livid. I knew that he could not be held responsible for his actions but I was angry this was happening. I did not show it but this was the final straw for me. Little did I know at that stage that he too had reached the same point. We went to the bank and got his finances sorted temporarily. He had very little to live off for 12 days, but he assured me it was enough. I reluctantly left him. I was divided by the desire to stay and look after him and also my own sense of having had enough and needing to get away from it.

I phoned the social worker and left a message with her informing her of what had happened and pointing out that this was a safeguarding issue. I asked her to call me when she received my message. She never did. Tom also told the police at the local community hub later that day. They were so concerned that they called Betty and Tom in for a meeting with the housing officer on the 20th June. They arranged for Tom to sign a tenancy restriction notice that was placed outside Tom's house. This denied legal access to some of Tom's acquaintances on the grounds of arrest if they were found in the property. Tom was hesitant about this idea, but housing made it clear that without it he would be evicted as they could no longer tolerate the people living in the property. The police also raised a safeguarding alert about Tom at this stage and arranged for a multidisciplinary team meeting to be held the following week, with a follow-up meeting to take place with his GP and Adult Social Care on 14th July. Tom did not make it to this meeting.

I am aware that in the last few weeks of Tom's life action did, finally, start to be taken to get him some help. However, it was far too little too late. Also, as Tom's advocate, I knew next to nothing about the things that were taking place. I would only find out two years later when the Safeguarding Adults Review into Tom's death was made available to us as a family. Adult Social Care had paperwork from that time which shows Tom had a review with them where he stated he did not want rehabilitation services. This may have been true by then, but I still maintain that had he received an assessment much earlier, and had he been supported by his advocate, then he would have agreed to go. He needed someone in that meeting to explain things to him and be there for him. Perhaps then things would have been different. This assessment report also stated he was at risk of financial abuse because of his living arrangements. By that time he had already experienced abuse and this had not been documented.

On Wednesday 25th June, I received a phone call from my best friend telling me that her mother had tried to take her own life and was at the nearby hospital. I rushed over there. Her mother had suffered from mental health problems for many years and there had been multiple incidents of attempted suicide. I remember sitting there with my friend at the hospital feeling remarkably calm. It did not really occur to me at the time, but my experiences with Tom had led me to a point where crises, even of the life-threatening type, were simply an everyday occurrence. My friend's mum recovered and was discharged from hospital on the Friday. I went over again that day to visit my friend and check how she was managing. I remember we sat in her lounge comparing our respective situations. She said to me that she felt awful for saying it but that one of the worst things about the situation with her mum was the uncertainty. She said that she did not want her mum to take her own life but she was fed up with the constant drama of it all. I completely understood. I think she thought I would be shocked but, instead, I simply agreed and said that I felt the same about Tom. I even said 'I just wish that if he's going to do it, he would just get on with it and put us all out of our misery'. This may sound incredibly harsh. I am also not proud of what I said. But I did mean it, and looking back I still do. I was exhausted of living a life for someone else. I was exhausted by fighting with organisations who did not know how to help or did not want to help. I was tired of fighting for a person's life when that person had long ago given up himself. I was tired of never being able to simply go home and sit down without worrying about when the next phone call or knock at the door might come. I was just tired of it all. Of course, little did I know how poignant my words would become. Only three days later Tom took his own life. My brother always did have a dark and twisted sense of humour.

On the afternoon of the 30th June, Betty, as frantic as I about the situation, emailed Adult Social Care yet again pleading for help. She impressed upon them, yet again, how unstable Tom was and how she feared he 'would end up dead in a ditch somewhere'. She copied me into the email, which she sent around 1pm that afternoon. Little did either of us know that he was already dead.

At around 5pm that afternoon a policeman arrived at our door. I answered the door and could see he was holding a piece of paper at his side. It had my brother's name written on it. I looked at it and saw the name before he had a chance to move it behind him. I remember laughing and telling him he had better come in before he had even had a chance to say anything. I had assumed that Tom had got himself into yet more trouble, or something had happened with the people at his flat. Despite the warning we had, I was not entirely expecting what we were about to be told.

The police officer came in and asked who I was. I told him and he said he was here to see Betty. I showed him through and I think I said something along the lines of 'what's he done this time then?' The police officer looked surprised and also very hesitant. He told us as gently as he could that Tom was dead, that the police had found him in his flat and tried to resuscitate him but that their attempts had been too late to save him. I remember Betty nearly losing her legs from under her and I put my arm out and guided her to the sofa to sit. I was in shock. I could not take it in. At that moment I heard my partner come in the backdoor with my 2-year-old son. I excused myself from the room, shut the door behind me and told my partner to keep my son occupied until I came to get them. He could see by my face that something was very wrong. I was able to say in a matter of fact manner that Tom was dead. I went back into the room with Betty who had clearly been asking lots of questions about what had happened. I do not know if this is a normal reaction but I did not want to know. I was not interested in what had happened. Tom was dead, that was really all that mattered. From what little I had taken in the police thought that it was suicide, although there would have to be an inquest. I wrongly assumed he must have taken an overdose. This seemed the most logical thing to have happened given his previous behaviour.

I then started to focus on the tasks that lay ahead. My sister Anna had to be told. I had to phone work. I had to let Jenny know. I phoned work first and I remember my colleague being really shocked that this was the first thing I had thought to do. In hindsight I was probably in shock, but I also think having had to deal with so many crises, you start to learn how to be practical about things too. Then I phoned Anna. I actually do not recall this phone call. I know I made it but could not tell you now what I said. Anna told me that when I phoned that afternoon she had just got back from work. She says she remembers the childminder was there and she was stood in her dining room. She remembers being 'gob-smacked' by the news. She says that she always knew it would happen one day and that there was a good chance he would take his own life and, certainly, would not reach old age. But, like me, she was in shock despite it not being a particular surprise.

After phoning Anna, I knew Jenny would have to be told. In the seven months since Tom had left Jenny's they had drifted apart, but Jenny still loved him dearly. Tom had gone so far down the rabbit hole of his drug and alcohol use that he rarely responded to her attempts to contact him, but I knew she would be devastated. I did not know how I was going to break this to her. I turned up at the house, having phoned on my way to ask if it was ok if I popped in as I was in the nearby area and could do with a quick chat. I did not want to have to tell her over the phone.

When I arrived at the house, Jenny and I chatted for a little while before she turned to me and asked me why I was there. She said that she was aware there must be a serious reason for my sudden visit. She had not been at all fooled by my attempts to make it seem as normal as possible. I told her what we had just heard and I remember her letting out this low moan. One of the consequences of Jenny's own brain injury was that she was unable to cry. She did not need to. The moan she gave out sounded like the kind of noise a wounded animal makes. I could tell how much it hurt her and I could not stop crying. Up until this point I had not allowed my own grief to hit me. Jenny's carer had been quietly waiting in the kitchen, pretending to be busy with some jobs while we had chatted. I had told her prior to speaking to Jenny that I had some bad news and Jenny was going to need support. She too looked very distressed. She had known Tom well from when he had lived at the property and was clearly upset by the news.

It was not until I returned later that evening that Betty told me about the real circumstances of Tom's death. Tom had hanged himself in a modification to the way he had described to me nine months previously. Tom had been suicidal all that time despite the number of health and social care professionals who had told us otherwise. Nine months down the line he had finally found a way to make it happen. I was never going to see my brother again.

Reflections

In the following chapter I will go on to describe the process of Tom's Safeguarding Adults Review that was opened after his death. I felt it important to separate this part of the story off as it stops being about Tom's story and is more about what happened to us as family survivors of brain injury. Yet it is important to reflect here on the 'learnings' that can be taken from Tom's case. As such, rather than providing my own personal reflections, I will instead report the professional reflections of Margaret Flynn, the chair of the Safeguarding Adults Review, who drafted the final report. I will add to this my own personal perspective on her points and then end with some of the recommendations that were outlined in the review. For those who want a more detailed account of these please see either the Safeguarding Adults Review (Flynn, 2016) or the article I wrote about the case (Norman, 2016).

Communication and information sharing: One of the key issues raised in the Safeguarding Adults Review was the lack of information sharing between, and within, organisations, and the lack of communication between different professionals. Adult Social Care had little contact with Tom post-injury, but as a recipient of Adult Social Care funding he was under their remit. Yet they were unaware of most of the events that were taking place within other organisations, such as the NHS. Furthermore, information was rarely communicated to us as Tom's family, and worse still to me as Tom's advocate. The failure of both the NHS and Adult Social Care to share key information meant that we were unable to support Tom, or advocate for him, leading to him failing to receive the care he needed. Tom's executive impairment meant that he struggled to understand his own difficulties and when he did understand he was unable to enact that information in the present (George & Gilbert, 2018). This is a common problem with people with brain injuries, but without advocacy it is one of the 'hidden disabilities' associated with brain injury that is so often missed (Moore et al., 2019).

Another failing in Tom's care was a lack of multidisciplinary team working. Tom had a severe TBI and was a substance user. He was also displaying signs of mental illness. Although he was assessed by the community mental health team as not having a mental health condition, this information was gathered without a wider understanding of Tom's other difficulties.

The poor interactions Tom experienced with various services can be summed up as being a categorical failure to appreciate the biopsychosocial model of health (Engel, 1980). This model highlights how biological and psychological factors can combine with environmental factors to influence individual's health. In Tom's case, the neurological damage caused by his TBI, alongside his mental health issues, substance abuse and social deprivation, both prior to and after his injury, led to a distinct vulnerability. At no point was this identified by the organisations working with him. Instead, each 'difficulty' Tom was experiencing was viewed in isolation, meaning that the organisations involved often missed the bigger picture.

Mental Capacity Assessment: The Mental Capacity Act (2005) provides guidelines to help support individuals with reduced mental capacity to make their own decisions. The Act is designed to protect and empower individuals. The premise of the Act states that individuals should be assumed to be capable of making their own decisions unless it is proved otherwise through a Mental Capacity Assessment. The Act also highlights that just because a decision may be viewed as unwise, it is not necessarily grounds for diminished capacity. Whilst this is an important point, in the case of Tom, he was endlessly making 'unwise' decisions both in terms of lifestyle choices and with regards to his care. Yet at no point was an assessment done, nor was there any suggestion from health or social care professionals that Tom may have difficulties making certain best-interest decisions for himself. I strongly believe that Tom had such capacity issues, at least towards the end of his life.

Safeguarding and risk management: During Tom's post-injury years, there were many occasions when safeguarding alerts or risk management assessments should have taken place. There were safeguarding alerts raised about Tom on four separate occasions, but the events above demonstrate that there were many other times when health or social care professionals should have been considering risk assessments and safeguarding. Yet these were not pursued. It is my belief this was primarily on the basis that Tom was viewed to have made a 'lifestyle choice' to do the things he did.

Echoing the recommendations from the review, it is my belief that the NHS and Adult Social Care need to work together to ensure information about vulnerable adults is routinely shared for the better management of their care. They often have complex needs and must be looked after by specialist multidisciplinary teams (Holloway, 2014). Organisations need to take a more active role in case management for individuals with TBI. There needs to be one individual accountable for information sharing and to act as a conduit for support, care and signposting for individuals and their families. Adult Social Care need to undertake regular specialist assessments to monitor the health and wellbeing of individuals with TBI (Holloway & Fyson, 2015). It is also imperative that health and social care professionals receive better training in understanding the difficulties associated with TBI, particularly with regards to mental capacity, dual diagnosis and the role of executive impairment.

Routine involvement of families is crucial in the care of those with TBI to circumvent the difficulties caused by lack of insight due to executive impairment. Furthermore, because individuals following TBI have residual intellectual capacity, there is a very real danger that they can present as being capable of making complex decisions (Holloway & Fyson, 2015; Moore et al., 2019). The advocacy role must be taken more seriously; family or advocate involvement is crucial to ensure cases of diminished capacity are not overlooked. Below is a reflection from one of the managers of Headway Somerset at the time of Tom's attendance (Professional reflection 6.1).

Professional reflection 6.1: Reflection from Louise Hawkins, Headway manager.

Helplessness is the primary word that comes to mind whenever I remember Tom, which I do frequently. There was something about the wholesale systematic failure of the professional infrastructure that we all assume is there to catch us when we need it that stays with me. Through absolutely no intention on Tom's part, he found himself the victim of a set of circumstances that meant he did not fit neatly into any one professions' area of expertise or responsibility, apparently.

I met Tom when he was still in a long-term and relatively secure relationship, where he had a role and an identity. He and his partner had their ups and downs and we regularly had discussions about 'rules' that seemed ridiculous to him; these were good humoured and interesting discussions and I used to enjoy the debate, as did he. Tom had a sharp intellect and enjoyed games that challenged him. Unfortunately, this worked against him when assessed by some professionals, who judged him as having the capacity to make quite complex life decisions, when in fact he would often forget the context of the discussion or react without reflection. Tom came to the centre to support his partner and never saw himself as wanting or needing support from Headway. However, the regular contact we had allowed confidences to be shared and support to be offered in an unobtrusive way. This worked well. We were a safe place. In the end that became more challenging when we moved premises, due not to any significant change on Tom's part initially, but because of the protocols of use for the community centre room hire, which had a zero tolerance policy for alcohol and substance use.

We tried many times to identify where support for Tom could be found. In our experience he spent his whole time being pushed between agencies, with no statutory agency wanting to take the lead. Individual people tried to work within the systems they were constrained by but, at the end of the day, we were told that Tom was making poor life choices and that he understood the consequences. Whilst I agree that Tom enjoyed his lifestyle for a while, in the end he was lost and confused by the decisions being made around him and had no idea how to conform so that he could get the help he badly needed.

Sadly, Tom's experience, whilst unique in a way (as Tom himself was), is not an isolated example of people falling out of the safety net (see Case study 6.1). I have worked, and still do, with many clients who have struggled to be heard, listened to and understood, and who have ultimately been blamed for their own circumstances. There appears to be little or no regard for the long-term consequences of sustaining a brain injury and the impact that may have on rational thinking and executive functioning.

Case study 6.1: RP safeguarding

RP was a 27-year-old male who was diagnosed with a brain tumour during childhood. RP underwent surgery to remove the tumour, resulting in his subsequent acquired brain injury. RP was unemployed and lived at home with his mother and brother in a small village. RP had a small friendship group but they all worked or did not live close by.

As a result of his brain injury, he struggled with a variety of cognitive difficulties, including executive skills such as planning and organising, motivation and initiation, memory problems and emotional difficulties.

RP's mother approached Headway Somerset for possible support for him and his family. RP was referred to Adult Social Care for an assessment and received funding for 1 hour 1:1 programmed rehabilitation per week. This funding did not allow for transport. RP's GP was not particularly supportive and required RP to obtain fitness to work certificates regularly, which caused a number of problems with the job centre. RP had several jobs in the past, however none of these have been long standing due to RP's cognitive impairments. RP had a job coach at the job centre who he was having regular meetings with. RP was working with an employment consultant, however his apparent lack of engagement led to a discontinuation of this service due to perceived lack of commitment. Consideration into RP's cognitive impairments needed to be given in order for RP to be successful in seeking employment. RP had also been referred for funding to complete further adult learning, however he missed several appointments with his advisor. If successful, this could have helped increase RP's self-esteem and motivation to find employment.

RP benefits from a flexible approach, as his ability to engage in support fluctuates. However, this is a difficult concept for non-brain injury specialists who often do not have appropriate insight into the everyday challenges of living with a brain injury and, therefore, are unable to successfully work with brain injury survivors.

RP reports feeling low in mood at times and has expressed negative thoughts about the value of his life. He struggles to think to the future as he feels he might not have one as a consequence of his brain tumour. As a result, RP and his mother report that he has become more withdrawn and distant, struggling to maintain quality friendships. This is likely to have a further detrimental impact on RP's wellbeing as he becomes more and more withdrawn. RP has reported low self-esteem and we are currently exploring ways for his confidence to be increased. With ongoing support RP is managing his benefits payments, although is still struggling to access learning or the workplace, which are high priorities for him.

RP had been on the waiting list for Talking Therapies for some time and eventually managed to arrange an appointment. Unfortunately, RP discontinued the service after only three sessions as he did not feel he was 'clinically depressed' and, therefore, did not need the service. RP does not appear aware of how his mental health is likely to be impacting on his everyday life. There are concerns regarding RP's long-term mental health and also how this will impact on his daily living and those around him.

RP has previously lived independently, however, as a result of missing several benefits appointments due to poor planning and organisation skills, as well as poor money management, this was unsuccessful and RP had to return to living with his mother.

RP is heavily dependent on his mother to manage his diary, important paperwork, and to motivate him to get through the day. Despite the 1:1 input from Headway and the use of external strategies, RP is lacking the ability to take more responsibility for himself. Adult Social Care seem to be of the opinion that support services should be time-limited and that he should have achieved optimum independence by now.

Chapter 7

The impact of suicide following traumatic brain injury

Tom's death occurred on 30 June 2014. Despite the beliefs of the organisations to which he was known, he took his own life and he did so through a modified version of hanging, just as he had stated to me that he would nine months previously.

The aftermath of Tom's death was devastating for us as a family, even though it was far from unexpected. In the first few days, we were all in shock. It is a strange situation to be in when you feel shock yet are not surprised by what has happened. On some level it was so expected and yet the fact that it had actually occurred seemed unreal. The first days were spent trying to sort out what little was left of Tom's 'estate'; notifying benefits agencies, closing bank accounts, getting an interim death certificate. We would have to wait a long time before a formal death certificate could be issued.

One of the worst tasks that immediately faced us was having to collect Tom's belongings from his bedsit. Tom had only a few meagre possessions that were worth keeping so we agreed with the council that we would check for anything of sentimental value and then they would dispose of whatever was left. The woman from housing was sensitive but forthright with me on the phone; Tom's dwellings were in a terrible state and they would need to send the clearance team in before they could make it habitable again. She also warned me that what we would encounter was not a pretty sight and tried to dissuade us from going at all. I was well aware of Tom's living arrangements at his previous address towards the end so was somewhat prepared for the state that would meet us. I did, however, try to dissuade Betty from going along with me as I was fearful about the emotional reaction it would elicit in her. In the end though we both went and I suspect she actually fared better than I did.

Going to his home was incredibly painful. On entering the bedsit, Tom's wheelchair had been left in front of the door. This was wholly unexpected and chilling, as he had used his wheelchair to enact his own hanging. It was such a surreal feeling seeing this object that I was so used to being part of him and now viewing it as the device that ended his life. This is the sort of scene family members should never have to see. The floor of the bedsit was covered in clothes and belongings, with hardly an inch of carpet showing. There were used needles scattered amongst the mess, which made it difficult and dangerous to look for anything to salvage. One of the most horrifying sights was the shower. It was piled high with bedding and clothes to such a degree that nobody could have used it for showering in the whole time Tom had been there, which had been about two months. This was testament to the level of self-neglect he had reached towards the end of his life. We collected the few belongings we wanted of Tom's, grabbed his near-infamous top hat and tails to dress him in for his funeral and left. We had to buy him new pants and socks as we could not find anything usable at the bedsit!

Planning the funeral was hard. Reflecting back on it now, I think we were all simply going through the motions. It was not a lavish affair; it was an 'off-the-peg' funeral. I look back now and feel we did Tom a disservice. We wanted it all to be over and perhaps in the rush for that, we did not take the time to celebrate his life at all. Perhaps that was because neither he nor we felt it was something worth celebrating. I think there was also a sense of stigma surrounding the funeral. While I have never ascribed to the view that suicide is in any way a 'sin', I think perhaps we picked up on a general sense that this was something that was best dealt with quietly and without fuss; that there should be no standing on ceremony.

The views of others became apparent to me soon after Tom's death. I learnt the hard way that there are many people out there who struggle to listen to grief and would rather shut it down. This happened to me on several occasions; I would start to discuss Tom and his death and would find the conversation being moved on rapidly. While I suspect this is common when people die, I think it is even more common in the case of suicide as people simply do not know what to say. One of the strangest moments I encountered was from a family member of my partner's. Some weeks later she apologised for not having sent me a sympathy card but stated that another family member had advised her that it was not 'appropriate' to send one. I was somewhat confused by this statement and could not understand why suicide meant that I did not deserve an expression of sympathy from others.

I do not know how Betty and Anna felt during this time or whether they experienced similar feelings of their grief being dismissed, but it was certainly something I felt deeply. I remember within days of Tom's death passing a friend of Betty's on the street. She told him what had happened and he was deeply sympathetic towards her. He then turned to me and simply said 'look after her, she needs you with what she is going through'. While I appreciate that, as Tom's mother, her grief may have been more intense, I remember feeling very side-lined by the comment, as though my own grief was being disregarded. This was particularly poignant given the time I had invested in caring for and supporting Tom in the years since his accident.

Tom's funeral took place on 12 July 2014. It was at the beginning of the following week that Betty and I attended a meeting with Adult Social Care. This meeting had been arranged prior to Tom's death. The plan had been to have a safeguarding meeting to discuss how best to support Tom moving forwards. While we appreciated that such a meeting was unnecessary, it had not been formally cancelled and we took the view that it would be a good opportunity to 'debrief' with the organisations involved. To say that they were surprised at our arrival would be an understatement. When we arrived one of the representatives from Adult Social Care informed us that what was taking place was a private meeting with the organisations and professionals involved and we were not meant to be present. The police representative took a different view and stated that he felt we had every right to be present at the meeting. On that note, we were invited in. The people round the table introduced themselves and offered their condolences. Tom's social worker said 'we are ever so sorry, but we just did not know this was going to happen'. This was a phrase that will stick with us for as long as we live. I remember Betty turning on her and saying 'well WE did and we told you many times it would'. The social worker was left speechless and the exchange set the tone for the meeting. We were not there to be confrontational, but there was a sense that some of the organisations were still not taking responsibility for the role they had played in Tom's death, or in the grief we were now experiencing. I did not want to make enemies of these people but I was full of anger and so was Betty. The response was typical of the sheer indifference that we had experienced over the preceding year.

Everyone finds the funeral of a loved one hard, and for most it is the quiet that descends afterwards that can be the worst of times. For us, the silence did descend but it was accompanied by an expectation of the fight that was yet to come. This meeting with Adult Social Care and the other organisations was the beginning of yet another long battle; the battle for justice. At the meeting in July, it was alluded to that there would be some kind of investigation into Tom's death and Betty and I waited in anticipation for this, both of us determined to fight as hard as necessary to ensure those responsible were held to account; Tom may have been the instigator of his own death, but there were many who were equally culpable.

In October 2014, stage one of our fight began with an email from Adult Social Care informing us that there was to be an internal review into Tom's death and that somebody would be in touch with us to interview us about what had happened. I remember being angry that they considered an internal review to be adequate, but it was something. Finally, in January 2015 we received another email from Adult Social Care requesting an interview with both myself and Betty. This interview was the point at which things started to change. Two professionals from Adult Social Care arrived at our home and spent nearly two hours talking to us about what had happened to Tom. It was evident from their faces that they were unaware of most of the detail we were giving them. I was grateful that they both acknowledged that we had been let down as a family and that Tom had been let down as a recipient of Adult Social Care. On leaving, they confirmed that there was every chance that the review would be upgraded to an independent Serious Case Review, or Safeguarding Adults Review as it would later be known. The process started in March 2015 when a chair was appointed to launch the review. By this stage the internal review had been completed and to our disappointment no action could be taken as Tom's social worker had retired early prior to its completion. The findings, however, were clear; Tom had not received the care he was meant to receive. It would be November 2015 before the review process finally began and we could not hold an inquest into Tom's death until after the review was complete because the outcome was needed before the coroner would proceed. To use the Americanism, this did not allow for a state of 'closure'.

By May 2016 the review process was complete. We had experienced only minimal contact with the review team and Adult Social Care in that period, but we had been kept updated about the progress. When the report was released to us, we were ambivalent. We finally had the result we were looking for; independent verification that Tom had been let down. But the Safeguarding Adults Review made for difficult reading and simply opened up old wounds that, by this time, we were all keen to let heal. On the completion of the report the plan was to release the findings publicly, but this was not to be. The coroner at this point reminded everyone involved that the findings of the review could not be made public until the inquest had been completed. So, in June 2016 we had to start the process all over again as the inquest was launched into Tom's death.

Meanwhile, I was asked if I would be prepared to be involved in a training event for NHS staff and social workers in the local area, providing the details of Tom's case and what had happened to him in the 20 years since his injury. In June 2016, I stood up in front of over 100 people and, for the first time, told the long story of Tom's life and death. I had never told the story in its entirety and, although there were aspects of it that were cathartic, it was also one of the hardest things I have ever had to do. It was also a day that was tainted by the realisation that, despite my heartfelt words about what had happened to Tom, there were people there who would not or could not comprehend. I refer the reader to the story given in the professional reflections section in Chapter 5.

The inquest into Tom's death opened in June 2016, two years after his death. This alone is difficult for a family who are looking to draw a line under the death of their loved one. But here we were about to start our next battle for justice for Tom. The inquest hearing was eventually set for early December, with the coroner booking in two days of hearing due to the complexity of the evidence that would have to be presented. For those who have never undergone an inquest, it is an interesting process, particularly where suicide is involved. An inquest is purely designed to determine the cause of death. In Tom's case this was entirely apparent; Tom had hanged himself. Yet the inquest was important to ascertain whether recommendations were needed by the coroner to ensure best practice in the future. I now have learnt that receiving a 'ticking off' by the coroner at the end of an inquest is something most health and social care organisations would rather avoid at all costs.

So as a family we started to prepare for our two days in court. While the review had been more important in many respects for getting justice, we had been generally absent from the process, except for private interviews with the chair. This was our chance to go to court and speak in public about the shortcomings of Tom's care. In order to do that, however, we had to sift through years and years of NHS and Adult Social Care records trying to pick out key pieces of evidence or key shortcomings that would demonstrate our point; that Tom had not experienced adequate care. One of the earliest stages of this was to read the coroner's report from Tom's autopsy. While there was nothing surprising in there, the details about his hanging were graphic and left very little to the imagination regarding the way in which Tom died.

During the autumn of 2016, Betty and I worked our way through these documents for the inquest. In November 2016, my youngest son, aged just 14 months, developed pneumonia and then sepsis and ended up in intensive care at the local children's hospital. Once he was out of the woods, I spent a long time sat by his bedside in the hospital watching him sleep while trying to absorb the case files that Adult Social Care and the health authority had on Tom. In early December, a day after my son was discharged from hospital, Betty and I immediately started the two-day inquest. It was a surprise to find myself almost cross examined at the coroner's court. While the barrister for Adult Social Care did tread carefully, I got the distinct impression that he was attempting to discredit my version of events; that Tom was in fact capable of making decisions for himself. This was made all the more surprising given that the Safeguarding Adults Review had strongly criticised this view.

It was a gruelling two days and Betty and I sat by as various pieces of evidence were unearthed, most of which seemed to very much support the findings of the review; that there had been no clear care plan for Tom and a lack of considered assessment of his needs. At the end of the second day the coroner passed his verdict; death by suicide. The organisations concerned must have been relieved that the coroner did not feel the need to pass any more comment on them but merely stated that he supported the findings of the Safeguarding Adults Review about the failures in care and that it was unclear whether changes in their practices would have led to Tom not taking his own life. This was a fair verdict; it would have been less likely that he would do so, but there was no certainty.

The worst aspects of the inquest for me personally were the 'apologies' that I received from the organisations. A woman representing Adult Social Care offered her apologies for what had happened but immediately followed it up by stating that she still held the view that Tom had capacity to make his own decisions. Given that the review process had taken over six months and the inquest process had then taken a further six months, it seemed incredible that this view could still be held. The representative from the NHS trust also came over and offered his condolences. To this day his exact words remain with me: 'the problem with your brother's case was that we just don't see people like him. I have worked in substance use and mental health for 20 years and I have never seen anyone with both issues and a brain injury'. I responded that this suggested a fundamental lack of understanding of the area and that the literature suggested that he had, in fact, seen plenty of patients just like my brother but that he had not known what he was looking for. He seemed surprised at my response but I did not feel he took my words on board; there was a sense that for all the findings of the review, we were wrong and they had in fact performed perfectly reasonably throughout.

This somewhat ignorant view is one that has remained ever since. After the inquest we had to wait until June 2017, after the completion of yet another general election, before the findings of the review could be made public. In June, there was a brief but fervent media frenzy about the findings and a lot of apologies were bandied about. This was short-lived. The local council scrutiny committee discussed the case in July 2017 and concluded that they needed to ensure that safeguarding processes were reflecting the teachings of the review. A friend of mine who sits on the local council insisted I be invited to the meeting to share my experiences and my professional viewpoint as a trustee of the local Headway group. I was not invited. I did attend the meeting but only because this person moved heaven and earth to ensure that I was there. Sadly, in the two years since the review was published, we have seen many similar clients in Headway and have made multiple safeguarding alerts to the local authority and yet these individuals generally do not seem to be viewed as at risk or vulnerable.

Despite my lack of confidence in the changes that have been made within my locale, I have continued to push the findings of the review to a national audience. I have done this for professional reasons; to try and protect the families and clients I have come in contact with. I have done it to try and protect future families and clients yet to come. I have also done it for my own personal reasons; I need to know that Tom's death was not entirely in vain. I know that in reality there will be plenty of 'Toms' and I know there will be plenty more sisters like me and Anna or mothers like Betty, and spouses or children who will experience the trauma and the grief that we encountered. I know that this is happening across the country every single day. It is only a matter of time before the next suicide takes place. In this way it feels somewhat pointless that I continue to do conference circuits and to write at length about Tom's story and of my own. And yet, for me, it brings a sense of purpose. Without this to hold on to I think the grief that I experienced, and am still experiencing five years on, would have been harder to bear; I have had somewhere to focus my efforts.

Reflections

Personal reflection

From my own personal perspective, Tom's death had come at a terrible time. Not that there is ever a good time for such a thing to occur. I was due to marry my partner at the beginning of August 2014, only five weeks after Tom took his own life. To this day I do not know how I made it through those weeks. Tom's funeral was in early July and my hen party was the very next day. Thankfully I had already decided to have a low-key event with a small number of friends and close family to celebrate with, rather than anything lavish. Yet I found myself chatting to my closest friends, at my hen party, about my brother's funeral and visiting my brother's flat. Few things in my life have ever felt so surreal. At the time I remember my husband-to-be suggesting we cancel the wedding, but it seemed so immoveable. We went ahead with the wedding more because I was unable to do anything different than continue on the 'autopilot' I was on. The same week that Tom died we not only collected the interim death certificate but we also collected a marriage registration.

I remember wandering through town about a week after the funeral looking for cosmetics for the wedding. I walked into a department store and the store assistant asked me if she could assist me. I remember explaining that I needed foundation for my wedding make-up. She looked like all her Christmases had come as once; before I knew what was happening I was in the chair being made up to look 'flawless'. While doing my make-up I remember her saying 'for a bride-to-be you don't look very happy'. I stared at her for a moment, unsure of what to say, and then explained as best I could that my brother had taken his own life two weeks before. I actually felt for her. The poor woman wanted the ground to swallow her up. She gave me so many freebies that day simply because she could not find the words to make it better for me. But at least she tried.

The wedding itself was a fantastic day and it would be unfair to suggest that Tom was the only thing on my mind. But he was there. Or more to the point; he wasn't. We left a glass of brandy by the bar sat upon a quote taken from a Pogues (Tom's favourite band) song, 'The Parting Glass'. This was an important gesture and it helped to feel that he was still part of the day. That and we had managed to get Jenny to attend the wedding. But there are no photos of my brother at my wedding because he was not there and the day was punctuated by pain as well as joy. Later into the evening, with a few drinks on board, I remember starting to talk to those around the table about Tom's death. I recall very clearly my husband's best man responding 'Aly this isn't the time or the place'. I remember being so angry that I was being shut down from talking about what I was going through on my own wedding day. People do not know how to handle death, let alone suicide.

As well as these memories of times where Tom should have been present, the other most difficult aspect of his death has been knowing what has been missed. Tom was never a fan of children and referred to them all as 'sprogs'. Yet despite this he had left an impression on my older son who would now never remember his uncle due to his young age. My youngest son would never know his uncle at all. These are the kinds of situations that are painful after the death of a loved one, but are made even more so by the thought that you can never truly explain to a young child why they are not there anymore. In the five years since Tom died, I have taken my boys with me to most crematorium visits to lay flowers, but I cannot explain to them that Tom wanted to end his life and decided to do so in such a brutal fashion. It will be years before they can even try to comprehend this. I know my nephews, Anna's children, have struggled to understand and they are much older than my boys.

After the wedding, there was a period of time to try and adjust to Tom's death. It is surprising how quickly life moves on. But for a long time I was haunted by disturbing dreams and thoughts about what had happened to Tom. In the early stages after his death, I took solace in the view that I had done everything I could for him so I need not feel any sense of guilt. But as time went on this safety net seemed to disappear thread by thread and I started to seriously doubt whether I really had done 'everything I could'. I started to think of all the things I could have done, all the people I did not contact, all the people I did not push hard enough, and over time I found myself experiencing a huge amount of guilt that I was, in part, responsible for Tom's death. If only I had done more, or done something differently, or fought harder, then maybe he would still be here today; maybe I could have managed to convince him not to give up for just a little bit longer. This sense of guilt experienced by loved ones following suicide is well documented in the literature (Shields, Kavanagh & Russo, 2017).

There were also the unhelpful thoughts about what it might have been like for Tom in his final moments of life. Did he suddenly regret what he had done? Did he want to change his mind but it was too late? How much pain was he in? And, quite selfishly, did he ever think about me and what this might do to me? As a psychologist I can accept that he was far beyond being able to consider me at that point, and I do not blame him for it. But as a person it is difficult to accept. There is nothing positive that comes out of this way of thinking but the spectre of suicide is something that lives with a family forever; those questions will never be answered, making it difficult to make meaning from the events (Shields et al., 2017).

Then there were the nightmares. For several months after Tom's death it was not unusual for me to dream that he was still alive. I would then wake up and for a brief moment not realise that it had been a dream. Then reality would hit me again; my brother was dead. This went on for some time and was probably one of the most horrific parts of the experience; it was like having to come to terms with what happened all over again. I remember one particular night having a very vivid dream that he was still alive and I was trying to save him. The dream kept looping so that every time I tried to do something, I would fail and Tom would end up dead. Rather than waking up, the dream would then start all over again. At one point Tom was sat calmly at a piano playing away while I was frantically trying to save him from some unforeseen danger. Tom never played the piano so I am not sure what the significance of this was, but in the dream I sat down beside him at the keys and he just looked at me with a small smile upon his face. I looked into his eyes and said to him 'is this really what you want?' He simply replied 'yes'. At that point I woke up and, once I had stopped feeling disorientated, I felt more at peace. I cried for a long time, but it was the response that I needed; he meant it and was at peace with his decision. I know as a psychologist that this was my own mind giving this to me and not a visitation by Tom from beyond the grave, but for all that, I still hold on to that dream now as a reminder that this was what he wanted. Yet still this does not stop me from having nightmares, even now, that I am back in that bedsit with him again trying desperately to stop him from taking his own life. Even now I find myself begging him to hold on a little longer, not to give up even when I know he did many years ago.

Despite these dreams, I have to admit that there is still a huge sense of relief. Living with Tom was really hard work. We were all living in a constant state of crisis; waiting for the phone to ring, for the police to arrive or for some difficulty to be addressed. The absence of this has made my life more peaceful despite the grief that I feel. This is a blessing but it is also a curse for it is associated with a huge burden of guilt; how could I ever possibly be relieved that my own brother took his life? I am relieved that I can focus on my own life and I can focus on that of my children's without the major distraction. When Tom died, other than the initial pain and anger at what had happened, the relief was one of my strongest emotions (see Case studies 7.1 and 7.2 for similar stories). Yet the relief was to be relatively short-lived. While we no longer had the crises to deal with, things certainly did not fall silent after Tom's death.

Case study 7.1: 'Iris'

Iris was 53 when she was hit by a car on a night out. She experienced multiple injuries, including a TBI. Iris survived her injuries and received two months of rehabilitation before being discharged home. It was advised that Iris should remain in hospital longer but she and her family believed that home was a better environment for her recovery. After six months at home Iris was managing well physically and her head injury appeared, at least to others, to be relatively minimal. It was around this time that the mood swings Iris had experienced since the accident started to become more intense and she started to show signs of both anxiety and depression. Iris became suicidal.

For the next three years, it was common for Iris to disappear from the home, often in a rage or deeply depressed. She would then send messages to her family stating that she was going to take her own life. Thankfully, Iris never did and eventually her suicidality started to subside. One of Iris' children reflected after this time that she reached a point of 'burn out' with Iris' behaviour. She expressed a sense of shame that she had found herself wishing that she would simply 'get on with it'. If Iris was going to take her own life, it would be better for all concerned if she did it sooner rather than later. While she did not want her mother to die, she was suffering burn out caused by her ongoing mental health problems. She had reached a point where she was unable to keep giving positive emotional support; a process known as compassion fatigue, which is common amongst professionals and family members who experience exposure to secondary trauma (Fortener, 2000; Lynch & Lobo, 2012).

Case study 7.2: 'Carol'

Carol has a degenerative neurological condition and has experienced multiple mini strokes. Since Carol's husband died she has felt depressed and suicidal. She has also accrued debts that her daughter has had to pay off. In the last five years, Carol has tried to take her own life on many occasions. Each time she has ended up in hospital and has been under the care of the crisis team. Carol has two children; Lisa and Paul.

Lisa reflected that after Carol's second suicide attempt and the third occasion of her accruing debts, she reached a point of hopelessness. Lisa talks openly about how she knows that Carol is not responsible for her actions; that she is mentally ill, but she is angry and hurt by what has happened to their family. Lisa struggles to cope with Carol day to day and has expressed that she wishes Carol 'would just do it [take her own life]'. As with the examples above, this is not because Lisa wants her mother to die. It is borne out of frustration, resignation and compassion fatigue from the stress she has been living with since her father's death. Lisa reflects that others find it difficult to understand how hard life is for her and she would never feel comfortable admitting to others that sometimes she has wished her mother dead.

Ambiguous loss and complex grief: When Tom first had his accident we were overwhelmed by a sense of grief at the idea that we might lose him. This grief then transitioned to one of ambiguous loss, as we had to learn to let go of the Tom who had been and try to learn to live with and love the Tom who had replaced him (Boss, 1999). When Tom took his life, this grieving process of over 20 years was finally allowed to come out; it could be expressed in its entirety. The nature of brain injury and the ambiguous loss that it brings makes the death of a brain-injured loved one different from the death of other loved ones. This is not to say that the grieving process is any worse or any better, just different. Equally, the death of a loved one to suicide brings about its own unique challenges in learning to live with the loss (Shields et al., 2017). Suicide still has moral connotations in our modern society and it is still a topic that many people feel unable to discuss (Sheehan, Corrigan, Al-Khouja & Stigma of Suicide Research Team, 2017). That makes the grief of a loved one following suicide feel all the more isolating (Kõlves et al., 2019). Furthermore, the distressing nature of deaths, or the circumstances surrounding one's death, by suicide leads to a barrier in the natural grieving process; this is often referred to as 'complicated' or 'complex grief' (Horowitz et al., 2003).

From my own personal perspective, I wonder whether the combination of the two is a very unique feeling indeed. I have missed my brother since he nearly died over 20 years ago. I have spent 20 years living with a person who nobody understood and very few people cared about. I now live with the memory of a man shunned by his lifestyle choices and the choice to take his own life. Tom's absence in my life is felt every day, even now. I still have to fight to suppress the thoughts I have about how he died. We as a family have to live every day in Tom's absence and live with the knowledge of what he did to himself. I try to take comfort in the knowledge that it was ultimately what he wanted and that in a life with no control over anything, he finally managed to end his life in a manner of his choosing. This perspective, however, is difficult to reconcile with my own sense of grief. And yet, as I have expressed before, there is a sense of relief that Tom is dead. His death marked the end of a long and ultimately pointless battle to preserve a life that only we seemed to consider worth preserving. It is hard for me to think of the amount of money and time that must have been invested into saving his life after the accident, only for the very same services to later turn their backs on him. From a ruthlessly economic perspective, this seems a waste of resources. It is also an unreasonable moral decision too; I am minded of the Chinese proverb that 'if you save someone's life you are responsible for it'.

When Tom was alive he hated the anniversary of his accident. He would always mark it by refusing to leave the house or engage with other people at all. He shut us out as family too. He was unable to appreciate that the anniversary was actually a very hard date for us too, not least because we had the memories of what happened that day. Yet as the years went on, it certainly faded for me. I would never have been able to forget that date but it seemed less and less relevant over time. Now that Tom is dead I find myself marking that anniversary more than I mark the anniversary of his actual death. This is, in part, because I find it difficult to think about Tom's suicide even now, five years on. But I also think that in some way, for me at least, the accident marked the day that Tom really died. In reality we lost him that day and we then spent 20 years fighting for the shadow of the man who used to be.

Reflecting back on the memories of Tom's funeral and the sense of stigma surrounding his death, I feel a degree of anger and I feel that in many respects my grief was robbed from me; I was not given permission to feel what I needed to feel. My sense now is that Tom was also robbed of a funeral befitting of someone who had fought so hard all of his life. But there was a sense that others did not view it in that way; that they instead viewed his life as an ongoing 'car crash' and that we were all better off without him. This is in stark contrast to how the death of a son or a brother should be observed. I will never know whether this feeling I have about Tom's death is accurate; whether others really did view it that way or whether this was my own interpretation. Certainly though, it has only really been my colleagues who have worked in brain injury who I have felt truly understood my loss or fully respected Tom for who he was. This is of interest given that only a small number of these people ever even knew him in life. This, I feel, highlights the uniqueness of our experience; brain injury is so poorly understood that only those close to it will ever be able to understand (Linden & Boylan, 2010).

Trauma: Tom's suicide has only added to my sense of trauma over the years. Added to the trauma of his accident and the years of living in a perpetual state of crisis, waiting for the inevitable calls for help. I have now added more traumatic memories; of Tom's self-neglect before he died, his words to me when he told me how he would take his own life, seeing his flat and his wheelchair in the doorway after he died. This, coupled with the intrusive images about how he died, has left an impact on me that I have no doubt will last forever. And yet I do still have a sense of relief that he is gone, which of course only adds to my sense of guilt and wishing I had done more for him.

The ongoing process of the review, followed by the inquest and then by the wait for the findings to be publicised, all had a traumatising effect too. It is akin to constantly picking at a scab so it is prevented from healing properly. It was three years of living on that treadmill before we were able to go back to what can be considered a 'normal' life. We were unable to gain 'closure'. The process of inquests generally have been noted to cause delayed acceptance from grief and have been described by family members as traumatising in many different ways (Biddle, 2003).

Perspective: Grief in any situation is experienced differently by each family member and for very different reasons; how close you were, how much involvement you had, and whether you feel guilt, sadness, anger or desire to celebrate the life that was (Kissane & Bloch, 1994). It is easy in situations of grief to make assumptions that everyone's perspective is the same. While there are likely to be shared views, there are often vast differences too (Griese, Burns, Farro, Silvern & Talmi, 2017; Kissane & Bloch, 1994; Sanders, 1980). It is also important to hold in mind the perspective of the loved one whose life was lost; how would they view the situation? This is particularly true of suicide. As such I have included below the perspectives of Tom (Box 7.1) as I imagine them to be and have given space for Anna (Box 7.2) and Betty (Box 7.3) to share their reflections on Tom's death and the impact it has had on them, before opening this up to a more professional viewpoint (Professional reflections 7.1 and 7.2).

Box 7.1 Tom's perspective

As I have discussed above, Tom's view of his life, and undoubtedly his death, were very different from mine. In Tom's mind the accident brought an end to everything that was enjoyable in life. He would never be able to ride a motorbike again, drive a car at high speeds or generally enjoy the freedom of a life lived his own way. Tom's accident took away his hope of a meaningful and intimate relationship. Once Faye had left he had no other intimate relationships. Even his relationship with Jenny was lacking in that respect; to him this was an important element that was missing from his existence. It made him feel like a 'cripple' as he would often tell us. He felt rejected and this deeply affected his already damaged self-esteem. Tom was stuck in the past. He was endlessly ruminating about a life that once was and a life that could have been. He could not stop to focus on the life that he could have. Without support he was never going to be able to view things in a positive light. Tom talked on many occasions about ending his life because he found his existence post-accident so unbearable. He often stated quite clearly that he wished that he had died. He certainly could not share our view that if it had not been for the accident he may well have been dead many years before (due to his risk-taking behaviour). Tom, in his eyes, had nothing to live for. Tom was plagued by this constant rumination and negative view of himself. This perspective is important. For all the blame that can be laid at the doors of others, ultimately Tom wanted his life to end.

Box 7.2 Anna's perspective

Anna reflects that her perspective on Tom's situation has changed over the years. Several years before Tom's death Anna and Tom lost contact. This was caused by a series of disagreements about his behaviour, culminating in Tom taking drugs in front of her children and being unable to appreciate why this was a problem. This resulted in Anna severing ties with him. Anna admits that, prior to the Safeguarding Adults Review, she had placed too much focus on Tom being a drug addict and not enough on the impact of his brain injury. She viewed him as refusing to do anything with his life and he simply needed to stop taking drugs. She viewed it in a similar way to many of the organisations surrounding Tom. Anna was disappointed with him and the fact he was not making more of what was on offer for him after his accident. She recalls the day centre he originally went to and his fondness for woodwork. She could not understand why he was not using it in the way he could or should.

Despite this view, Anna talked about the blow that the closure of the day centre was for Tom. She stated that 'his lifeline had been taken away'. Anna talked of Tom's relationship with Jenny and how it meant he had someone, but that this was not a stable relationship. He was gradually giving into his drug use and this reduced his ability to have a relationship. Anna admits, with hindsight, she was too dismissive of Tom's difficulties. She recalls an argument she once had with him. He told her how he 'wanted to feel the touch of a woman'. Anna dismissed this as she did not want to know about his sexual needs. He later wrote her an angry letter about how she had dismissed his feelings and called her a 'bitch' for not taking it seriously. Anna responded by writing an angry letter back telling him he did not have the right to say what he liked just because he had a brain injury. Anna now reflects that in many respects he did have the right but she did not realise it at the time. This was something she did not appreciate until after the Safeguarding Adults Review was released. This gave her insight into exactly how much, or how little, he was able to grasp.

Anna stopped seeing Tom because she did not understand and because he did not like children. Tom would only come round to her house when her children were in bed. When she took them round to Tom's place, his belongings would be everywhere and they could not be touched due to his obsessive nature. There was drugs paraphernalia everywhere that made it unsafe for children. She did not understand at the time that his brain injury meant that he could not help this behaviour. She treated him like an adult rather than an incapacitated one.

Anna reflected that she felt she did not try enough or understand enough. She feels that with hindsight perhaps she could have tried harder and things between them could have been different. Anna was very honest that there was a degree of selfishness on her part of not wanting to deal with Tom. She admitted that she did not know enough about brain injury, but also that she did not want to know or try as hard as she could to find out. She did not realise the impact the accident had on his brain; this was a realisation she would come to after her experiences with her own son who has autism. This experience has given her the sense that she could have treated him differently, had lower expectations of him and talked to him differently.

Anna reflected that, for Tom, he was in a better place after his death. Anna describes how lonely and sad he was; that he had nobody. She feels that for him it was the right decision despite how hard it might be for others. She said that she was never angry with him and was instead accepting of his decision; his life no longer had any meaning. Everything in Tom's life had been taken away or he had messed it up in some way or another. Anna's words were 'what an empty and lonely existence it must have been'. He was miserable and in pain; life was not fun anymore. Anna reflects that she cannot remember the last time Tom would have had fun. His drug taking was not fun; it was about self-medicating. He did not have any friends, just people who used and abused him.

Anna talked about how Tom's death impacted her. She feels it was less severe for her than for Betty and I because she had not seen him since 2008. She had grieved for him on several occasions throughout her life. The first was when she was a teenager and she lost the brother she knew when he started to 'go off the rails'. She grieved again when he had his accident and again when Faye left, which caused such a marked change in him. She then grieved again when she stopped seeing him. Because of this Anna felt she had already done a lot of her grieving by the time Tom physically died. Anna reflects that the impact must have been greater on me because I was so present in his life and he in mine, and I had been his advocate for so many years. Anna talked of the meetings I and Betty had sat through and the things that we had seen, and his gradual demise that Betty and I both had to witness. She reflects she was protected from all these things.

Anna described Tom's death as a shock; that he was actually physically gone; not present at all rather than just not present in her life. She also felt the shock of his suicide even though it was anticipated; Anna talks of the effect suicide has on people, that it is not something most people encounter. She says that people are shocked when you tell them your brother committed suicide. Anna then went on to talk about the factors involved in suicide; that Tom was male and depressed and a drug addict and had a brain injury. She says 'it is no wonder he took his own life'.

Anna finished her reflection by considering advice she may have for other families living with brain injury. Her response was to learn more about it. She reflects again that she did not know enough so she could not do enough. She then went on to state that she did not think she was the best person to give advice and that when it comes to bereavement by suicide, the experience is different for everyone. It will depend on the family connection as well as the individual. Anna concluded that the strange aspect of losing a sibling is that they are gone before their time.

Box 7.3 Betty's perspective

Betty was given the opportunity to reflect on her own feelings after Tom's death, but she struggled to articulate these clearly. What was clear from Betty's account was that she had been broken by the death of Tom, her first-born child. While Betty would never admit to it, Tom was always her favourite; her golden child. She had high hopes for what Tom would achieve and his life and death have been deeply distressing to Betty as his potential was never realised. It must have been difficult for Betty to accept that he had not, and would not, achieve all the things she would have wanted for him.

While Betty struggles to articulate emotion, her grief is palpable and was very much so in the early days and weeks after Tom's death. She struggled to part with many of Tom's belongings and held on to unusual gifts that he had given to her over the years. She made a collage of a collection of pictures of Tom and kept them on display along with his top hat. This was her way of showing her grief at losing her only son.

Betty shared my own sense of relief at Tom's passing. This was partly relief borne out of fatigue but also relief for Tom. She expressed to me on many occasions that at least Tom was now at peace, even if it is not what she would have wanted for him. She struggled with her own emotions surrounding Tom's death and, although she did not share these readily, she has expressed on several occasions that it has left her feeling suicidal.

Betty has observed some of the anniversaries since Tom's death (birthdays, anniversaries of the accident and anniversaries of his death) but she has not observed them as much as I have. It is difficult to know why this may be. Perhaps she finds it difficult to observe them and would rather distract herself with other activities. Whatever Betty might be feeling it is clear that this has had a profound effect on her, as anyone would expect from losing a child.

Mental wellbeing: I am constantly amazed and heartened by the more positive stories that exist for people following brain injury. While many struggle, there are others that see their injury as an opportunity to start again; to live a new life. This is also true for some family members too, who embrace the new person rather than becoming engulfed in the ambiguous loss for the person that is no more. This was not our experience of brain injury as a family, but I feel that Tom's death, despite its traumas, has brought about some positive growth for me. Not long after Tom died I decided to raise money for Headway Somerset by walking 43 miles over a weekend; a mile for every year of Tom's life. For months after Tom's death I would go on training walks on my own, often in some pretty atrocious weather (it was the winter in the UK after all). Those walks were very important for me. They gave me the space and the time to reflect on what had happened and to regain some kind of inner peace. They also gave me the energy to try to bring about a positive change. It was in those days when I walked that I made the active choice to ensure that I did whatever it took to stop this happening to too many others. It was also when I realised my need to seek professional help to manage my grief and, in some respects, the anger that I had surrounding both Tom's life and his death. Getting that help allowed me to invest new energy in supporting others.

I have subsequently been given the honour of being able to present Tom's story at multiple conferences, I have written an academic paper on the topic, and now I am writing this book. These all help to provide a form of therapy for me; a way of reflecting on and processing what happened to us as a family. The literature on therapeutic writing, as well as the literature on sharing personal stories, demonstrates the importance of expressing these accounts in order to be able to move forward with one's life in a positive manner (Niederhoffer & Pennebaker, 2002; Wright & Chung, 2001). It also allows me to feel as though I am making a difference, although I still have some anger at the organisations involved, anger at the lack of respect that Tom was given and anger at the lack of respect we experienced as a family.

The National Suicide Prevention Strategy (2012) clearly identifies that all family members of those who have taken their own lives should be offered psychological support, as they too are at increased risk of suicidality. I have been in various conversations with multiple organisations about Tom's death and I can safely say that nobody has ever offered therapy to me or my family. This was something that we all had to seek out for ourselves. This feels to me like a lack of respect, like it undermines how significant Tom's death was to us and the impact it had on our family. Generally, my experiences of professional organisations since Tom's suicide suggest to me a general lack of understanding of the impact of suicide on family members (Peters, Cunningham, Murphy & Jackson, 2016) and a lack of appreciation of the importance of family involvement in preventing suicide from taking place (Manuel, Crowe, Inder & Henaghan, 2018).

Professional reflection 7.1: Reflections from Dr Yasmin Drew,
clinical psychologist

Before working in the world of brain injury and neurological conditions I simply had no idea about the impact they can have. I suspect that this applies to most, which means that when brain injury happens, the person themselves, their loved ones and their friends are completely unprepared for the journey that lies ahead.

The neuropsychological sequelae of brain injury are well documented in literature, particularly the cognitive, physical and emotional consequences. With all of that to contend with alongside the natural suffering inevitable to living, it is unsurprising that brain injury can affect every aspect of a person's life, including their personal relationships, their work and the way in which they engage with what's meaningful to them.

For those where injuries are 'mild', they can often fall through the net into the gap that is known to exist within public healthcare. They go back to their lives with little to no input. In Tom's situation, he experienced an accumulation of these events that leaves me unsurprised that living a meaningful life became so much harder for him and, ultimately, left him feeling such despair that he felt his life was no longer worth living.

The hidden nature of brain injury can often mean that the expectations of an individual are not formulated in account of the cognitive and emotional deficits that can so often be present. Without specialist support, the individual and their loved ones (although not in all cases) are expected to navigate this minefield independently.

How have I seen this manifest in real life?

– A lost job because the 8-hour shifts are so fatiguing that they keep missing their morning alarm.
– Relationships breaking down because their mood has declined and they have withdrawn.

- An addiction because that feels like the most accessible way to cope.
- Unstable housing and finances because benefits forms are overwhelmingly difficult to complete.
- A frustrated family because they have tried everything and the individual is just not taking their help on board.

Eventually, a person becomes so far from who they were and, in some cases due to insight issues, they are not even aware that this is the case. For a family member, partner or friend, they are faced with feelings of loss and grief in spite of their loved one being very much alive. With little formal input available for families, these feelings are almost as hidden as the brain injury itself. I cannot imagine how much harder this was for Tom's family with the continuing stigma that surrounds death by suicide.

My own research has illustrated the difficulties children and young people face when their parent suffers an injury, regardless of severity. Other literature has found the same for siblings and spouses. In spite of this it appears that services are predominantly not available to support family and loved ones. I believe that this perpetuates the hidden nature of their grief and the isolation they can subsequently experience.

Over the course of the last decade, what has become glaringly obvious to me is that family and friends are undeniably important in the life of an individual after brain injury. I take the position that they are just as much of a priority in the picture as the person who has sustained the injury. This is not only with regards to the support they can provide the individual with the injury, but the support they themselves should receive for the turmoil that is so often presented after injury occurs.

What do I think might help? Ideally, all areas of the country would have a specialist brain injury team that can offer systemic support in acknowledgment of this. This is not to say that all relationships will be as they were after brain injury/onset of a neurological condition, after all, we cannot be who we were yesterday today. Rather, the process of adapting to life within this new and often scary context can be supported in a way that nurtures the opportunity to engage with a meaningful life, however that may now look.

It is said with deep sadness that we cannot change what has already happened for Tom and his family, but what should be fundamental is learning from the extremely distressing situation that he and his family have suffered through. Brain injury might occur within an individual but the consequences are system-wide, thus support must be positioned through a systemic lens.

Professional reflection 7.2: Reflections from Jo Clark-Wilson, brain injury case manager

When I read this chapter, it made me reflect on what I would do if this situation had occurred with one of my brothers. Living with the fear that your brother will take his own life is horrendous, but when this actually happens, can there be anything worse? Alyson describes her shock and then graphic details when reflecting on the actions she had to take in the immediate aftermath of her brother's suicide. She reflects on how her brother's death occurred shortly before her own marriage, thereby having the associations and conflicting feelings for her own special day. Coping with fluctuating emotions and grief after the death of any close family member is challenging at the best of times, but when being constantly reminded of the trauma in interviews, inquiries and inquisitions in court for over two years, how can you process grief when going over the same issues and reliving the experience? Is it reasonable or fair that family members should have to suffer the repeated traumas again and again? Alyson highlights how people who knew her mother assumed her role was to look after Betty, rather than acknowledging her own grief from losing her brother. This is an isolating experience. As a psychologist and a specialist in this area of work, it was expected that Alyson could take on this supporting role and manage her own grief. But this is so totally different, and as a personal experience it 'cuts to the core'. Alyson stated she never received any support – so effectively, they not only ignored her brother, but also herself. As a practitioner in brain injury, I share the experience that Alyson has, i.e. many people in statutory services do not listen, hear or recognise the issues associated with brain injury. It is shocking that even after an inquiry and report, which clearly specifies the actual issues that arose and the neglect her brother suffered, the professionals involved 'still could not get it'. I acknowledge Alyson's despair when the professionals made comments that highlighted their ignorance. As a practitioner in brain injury, this is a constant challenge. It is frustrating and irritating, as it not only places those with brain injury at risk, but it also causes their family members to feel isolated, burdened and under constant stress. Alyson is constructively supporting practitioners to understand the issues associated with brain injury, to make a positive difference to individuals with brain injury and their families' lives. In this period of austerity, will lessons have been learnt? I hope so.

Chapter 8

Final reflection on suicidality after brain injury

Community rehabilitation and integration

Throughout this book I have discussed the lack of community-based rehabilitation that was made available to Tom after he was discharged from hospital. From the moment that Tom was discharged the services surrounding him disappeared, leaving behind a chasm that could not be filled by us as a family. While there were many factors that influenced Tom's decision to take his own life, being denied basic support services no doubt had a major influence. While Tom had been deeply unhappy prior to his accident, his rumination on what had happened to him made his depression more severe at an early stage post-injury. With the right form of rehabilitation, Tom may have been able to develop a different perspective and have been able to see that the accident did not have to signify the end of life as he knew it. Tom was forced to take control of his own physical rehabilitation with little to no guidance from professionals on how to achieve this. It is unsurprising then that his gains were very gradual, took a lot of hard work to achieve and that he often injured himself further by engaging in physical activity that was ill-advised.

An ongoing concern of mine throughout Tom's time post-injury was the lack of occupational therapy he had received. While his cognitive, behavioural and emotional difficulties made it hard for him to engage in work post-injury, it is still my belief that he may have been capable of doing something more productive with his time than sitting around taking drugs. Occupational therapy started during Tom's time at a day centre where he started to learn woodwork, but more focused therapy may have been able to turn this into an interest that could have served as a protective factor. This potential was never recognised because the support simply was not there.

The biggest gap in service provision for Tom post-discharge was the absence of neuropsychology. Tom had extensive cognitive difficulties, particularly in relation to executive dysfunction. If he and our family had been given the opportunity to learn more about these difficulties and learn to manage them, things may have been very different.

Throughout the book, my colleagues have provided professional reflections on Tom's life. The fundamental similarity between all these accounts is the focus on the lack of services offered. This poor access started back when Tom was a child, with a lack of understanding and no services offered to support a child who may have been experiencing cognitive difficulties as a result of repeated head injuries. Even after his major accident, with a clear acknowledgment of the damage done to Tom's brain, services continued to be largely absent. It is important that this gap in services is accurately documented and considered by those responsible for organising them. Tom's case is not unusual but is in fact indicative of the experiences of many people with brain injuries, and their families, post-discharge (Odumuyiwa et al., 2019). As noted by the case manager in Chapter 4, these services may appear expensive on the surface, but the economic costs of cases like Tom's are far greater without adequate services. More importantly from a family perspective, it may have prevented Tom from taking his own life.

While the need for increased community rehabilitation is important, the need does not stop at these practical services. Rehabilitation is about helping individuals to regain pre-injury function where possible. This should not just be focused on physical improvement or return-to-work goals but, more widely, on regaining social and community integration. I described in Chapter 4 how Tom lost many of his friends after his accident. I say this again here not to point fingers at individuals who did not support him, but instead to highlight the human need for interaction. Tom's friends left because he was not the person he was before and this made it difficult for them to integrate the new Tom into their view of who he was. Yet, Tom was still capable of having social interactions and being part of the community. Despite Tom's somewhat anti-social behaviours, he was surprisingly well-liked. His neighbours liked him a lot, despite his drug-taking and shouting. They would often comment on what a lovely man he was. They could see past his behaviours to the man left beneath; a lonely soul who wanted to be loved.

Tom had two social outlets post-injury; Headway Somerset and the Halcon day centre. The Halcon day centre was closed due to insufficient council funds. This was such a shame for those who attended as it offered a community lifeline. Without Halcon, Tom would not have learnt woodworking skills and he would not have met some of the people he became friends with post-injury. He also would not have met Jenny. Without these social elements in his life, Tom's deterioration into psychological despair would have been significantly quicker. Headway Somerset was there to fill that void but the service was limited due to funding restrictions. These funding decisions can lead to intense social isolation for individuals like Tom (Headway UK, 2018a; Odumuyiwa et al., 2019).

Feeling isolated from the community and from social situations is a common complaint by individuals post-injury (Goranson et al., 2003). The literature on mental health tells us that this is a vulnerability factor for suicide (Leigh-Hunt et al., 2017). Yet these services are often viewed as inessential if they do not provide functional rehabilitation. Certainly, when Tom was finally told he would be unable to attend Headway, this had a profound influence on his already fragile self-esteem. He felt unloved, unwanted and uncared for. It also made him more determined to hold on to the drug-dealer friends he had acquired as they 'would not let him down'. This was not the fault of the organisation but did have a further negative impact on Tom's already vulnerable emotional state.

Mental health, substance misuse, brain injury and suicide

Tom's case highlights clearly the complexities of the relationship between mental health and brain injury. As discussed in the opening chapter, those who have experienced mental health difficulties are more susceptible to experiencing head injuries than those who do not have mental ill-health (Mainio et al., 2007). This is in part due to their vulnerability once they have developed mental health problems (Ponsford & Schönberger, 2010) but also due to the association between brain injury, mental health and adverse childhood experiences (ACEs; Ma et al., 2017). ACEs consist of a long list of negative experiences that children may be exposed to as they grow up, including domestic violence; parental abandonment; parental mental illness; physical, sexual or emotional abuse; and neglect (Felitti et al., 1998). In reality, most children reach adulthood having experienced at least one of these 'ACEs'. Yet, the literature on ACEs has long identified that individuals who experience four or more of these are far more likely to go on to develop mental health difficulties (Felitti et al., 1998). The literature has also indicated a link between ACEs and brain injury, partly due to the increased vulnerability that mental ill-health brings, but also due to the ACEs themselves, making it more likely that children will come to harm (Ma et al., 2017). Children may experience physical abuse or bullying at school that may directly lead to head injuries, but they may also experience neglect at the hands of their parents, which makes them indirectly more likely to experience head injuries (through unsupervised activity and risk taking behaviours; Ma et al., 2017).

The relationship between mental health and brain injury is further complicated by the neurological damage itself that makes individuals more prone to developing mental ill-health and suicidality after injury, even where no premorbid history was present (Dyer, Bell, McCann & Rauch, 2006). Overall, this makes those who have experienced a brain injury three times more likely to take their own lives than someone in the non-injured population.

Yet despite this well-documented and well-researched multidimensional relationship, Tom was not identified as being at risk of suicide by anyone other than his own family and his support staff at Headway Somerset. This is a shocking oversight. One that is further exacerbated by the statistics for suicide more generally; within our population, males in their early 40s are the most likely group (among non-injured individuals) to take their own lives. So, Tom was at the height of his statistical vulnerability and still no organisation took heed. He was not even considered to have a mental health condition despite the extensive evidence to the contrary.

A better understanding amongst health and social care professionals of the complex relationship between mental health and brain injury, and the additional vulnerability that offers to suicide, is of fundamental importance if we are to protect individuals from taking their own lives. Suicide prevention training is a staple of many health and social care professionals training, as is mental health awareness. Brain injury, on the other hand, is rarely included (Holloway & Fyson, 2015), nor is the complex interconnectedness between these variables. The links may not be clear to those outside the field and this can prove costly, as we as a family can testify.

Of further importance is the factor of substance misuse. As with mental health, the relationship between substance misuse and brain injury is a complex one. The literature demonstrates that those with a history of alcohol or substance misuse are more likely to go on to develop a brain injury (Ponsford et al., 2007). This may be due to falls, episodes of unconsciousness or from neurological damage caused by the substances themselves (Oddy et al., 2012). They are also more likely to experience road traffic accidents (Papalimperi et al., 2019). This alone should indicate the need for specialist services to treat substance misuse amongst those with brain injury. Furthermore, it is common for individuals with brain injury to go on to develop substance misuse or alcohol-related problems post-injury when they had no premorbid history of this (Gould, Ponsford, Johnston & Schönberger, 2011). The reality is that living with brain injury is challenging. People experience huge changes in who they are, in the things that they can do, in the ways people respond to them, and in the ways they feel about and see the world (Maas et al, 2017). Given these difficulties it is not surprising that some individuals take solace in substances. Add to this the executive impairments that can be present post-injury that can lead to increased risk-taking behaviour (Parry-Jones, Vaughan & Cox, 2004; Weil, Corrigan & Karelina, 2016) and one can see how substances become so appealing.

The increased propensity for substance misuse adds a further complexity to the relationship with mental health. Substance misuse, mental ill-health and high numbers of adverse childhood experiences are a facet of many survivors of brain injury (Ma et al., 2017). This makes the population incredibly vulnerable and at increased risk of suicide (Simpson & Tate, 2005). It also calls into question the issues of capacity and how able individuals may be to make best interest decisions for themselves regarding lifestyles, medical care and support services more generally. As highlighted in Chapter 6, the Safeguarding Adults Review concluded that Tom should have received a mental capacity assessment as there was good evidence to suggest that he was not able to act in his own best interests. And yet, this was not considered by the organisations involved. In fact, at Tom's inquest, despite the evidence for poor decision-making, Adult Social Care still maintained that they felt Tom had capacity. The lessons were not learnt here but maybe they can be elsewhere. There is an urgent need for improved training amongst health and social care professionals regarding the use of the Mental Capacity Act with adults with brain injury, particularly in relation to multiple unwise decisions (Moore et al., 2019). While the Mental Capacity Act states that unwise decisions are not necessarily a sign of a lack of capacity, repeated unwise decisions may indicate the presence of executive impairment, which may impede a person's ability to make such informed decisions (Jenkinson & Chamberlain, 2019; Moore et al., 2019).

When I am asked what would have made a difference to Tom, if I could make the changes necessary to ensure this did not happen to others, advocacy is a key word that comes to mind. At the heart of Tom's difficulties with organisations and services was a lack of advocacy. Tom was an individual who could articulate himself surprisingly well despite the damage that had been done to his brain. He had high residual intelligence and was certainly not stupid. These factors, unfortunately, tended to count against him in his interactions with services. It led professionals to assume that Tom was far more capable than he actually was. Crosson et al. (1989) highlights the problems that occur when an individual has 'intellectual awareness' into their disability but cannot necessarily use this information in a functional way. Being able to articulate one's needs or even being able to state how one might do things differently in the future tends to suggest an understanding that brings with it a lack of need for support, and a lack of need for capacity assessment (George & Gilbert, 2018).

Tom had such difficulties, but he also had some difficulties understanding his injuries too. He knew there was damage to his brain but he repeatedly underestimated the impact this had on his abilities. He would often say that he was 'brain damaged not hard-of-thinking' and while I could never have accused Tom of being 'hard-of-thinking', it is true to say that at times he did not have the intellectual awareness of his own difficulties. He could see that executive impairments were a problem for some people with brain injuries but he underestimated the impact this had on his own functioning. This, along with his difficulties in processing information in real time, meant that he was often left confused by conversations with professionals and failed to articulate his needs clearly. What he needed was an advocate. He had one – me. Yet, sadly for Tom, this was rarely acknowledged and acted upon. The 2014 Care Act now states clearly the need for advocacy if a person feels they need it or struggle to communicate their needs. I have little faith that Tom's situation would have been changed by this ruling because it still requires a professional to acknowledge advocacy may be required AND ask the question. With advocacy it is possible that maybe Tom would have been able to access more services that should have been available to him, and with advocacy he then may have been able to reconstruct a meaningful sense of self.

As well as formalised advocacy, one of the factors missing from Tom's interactions with organisations was a general involvement of his wider family. We would never have expected to attend every appointment but there were many conversations that took place where our input into Tom and his needs could have been insightful. This led to Tom being unable to access services but also led to frustrations for us as a family. Whenever we tried to be involved we found we were met with a wall of resistance; we were interfering in business that was not ours. Far from being overprotective or overdramatic, we generally allowed Tom to live his life the way he chose but we still found ourselves accused of trying to protect him from himself – from his 'lifestyle choices' that, as far as the services were concerned, were his right to make. This assumption was made without a full understanding of the extent of Tom's injuries and how these may influence his ability to make such choices.

Tom would have benefitted from a more cohesive and holistic model of care. At no time did any one professional take responsibility for Tom's case. This was something that was highlighted in the Safeguarding Adults Review (Flynn, 2016). Tom would no doubt have benefitted from a form of case management with one individual looking at his care needs and coordinating it, while ensuring that his 'voice was heard'. Tom would have benefited from improved information sharing about him and his conditions between organisations and across professionals to improve his quality of life. This may have been effectively coordinated by someone like a case manager. Had Tom received this form of care post-discharge, I feel there would have been a good chance of a more positive recovery.

Bereavement support post-suicide

Our experience of being side-lined in Tom's care continued after his death. The initiation of the Safeguarding Adults Review meant that we finally had the opportunity to express our side of the story and, more importantly, be heard. But otherwise we were largely ignored. There was limited acknowledgement of what we had been through as a family, and while there were some apologies, these were often followed by various caveats 'sorry but we still think he had capacity', 'sorry but we don't see cases like this'. Interestingly, nobody took an interest in how we were doing and how we were feeling – it was as though we did not matter, that our sense of grief was irrelevant. This is an important point to note because we were incredibly vulnerable at that time, some may argue that we still are, and yet our needs were not recognised.

The National Suicide Prevention Strategy (2012) laid down six action points for helping to address the growing problem of suicide across the UK. The document makes for an interesting read in light of the journey our family went on. Action 1 refers to the need to identify high-risk groups in order to reduce the risk of future suicidal behaviour. The document helpfully identifies that 'men are three times more vulnerable than women' and that 'men aged 35–49 are now the group with the highest suicide risk' (National Suicide Prevention Strategy, 2012). Tom was in this category. The guidance does not comment on brain injury but, even without that specialist knowledge, it would seem that when we expressed our concerns about Tom's behaviour to various organisations, someone should have taken more action. Furthermore, the guidance goes on to say 'Factors associated with suicide in men include depression, especially when it is untreated or undiagnosed; alcohol or drug misuse; unemployment ... social isolation and low self-esteem' (National Suicide Prevention Strategy, 2012). This could have been describing Tom specifically. As a vulnerable individual at a high risk of suicide he should have been the recipient of support services.

Action point 4 relates to the need to 'provide better information and support to those bereaved or affected by suicide' (National Suicide Prevention Strategy, 2012). This point is particularly important. The document highlights quite clearly 'Family and friends bereaved by a suicide are at increased risk of mental health and emotional problems and may be at higher risk of suicide themselves'. The document goes on to provide a list of helpful resources for signposting bereaved relatives to forms of support and counselling. In many circumstances one might argue that this would be easy to overlook. Unless a professional has specifically been told that a person's loved one died from suicide, they would not necessarily be privy to this information. Yet, in our case there were a wealth of organisations who were in contact with us who were all too aware of what happened to Tom – Adult Social Care, community mental health, the police, housing support, GP services etc. At no point did any of them signpost us to support. We were not even signposted to support during the inquest process, although arguably this may have been too late given that in Tom's case this did not take place until over two years after his death. It seems remiss that these organisations, having failed my brother so fundamentally, did not seize on the opportunity to support us as a family thereafter. The cynic in me is surprised that this was not a preferred course of action merely to keep us 'on side'.

Moving away from our personal experience, the National Suicide Prevention Strategy highlights some fundamental points that are necessary for reducing suicide risk. It is vital that high risk individuals are accurately identified and that the concerns of those around them are taken seriously. It is important that family members who are concerned that their loved one may be at risk of suicide are offered support, and that in the event of suicide these individuals are signposted to relevant support in a timely fashion. Health and social care organisations need to work harder to ensure that this support is in place and that appropriate signposting occurs. While the 2017 fourth progress report on the National Suicide Prevention Strategy outlines improvements in services, it also highlights that there is still a lack of suicide bereavement services nationwide. Interestingly, the document discusses a support group in Somerset that has been running since 2012 with positive effects. As a family member bereaved through suicide (and a psychotherapist in the local area), this is the first time I have become aware of this group that is on my doorstep. This raises the importance of signposting; people should not be left to find this information out for themselves. In our case, we all sought our own grief counselling at different points following Tom's death but that was not through signposting from organisations.

Suicidality following TBI: What we know from the literature

Tom's is only one case amongst a population of people who are vulnerable to suicide. Certainly it would be wrong to assume that what might have worked for Tom might have worked for others but, in the absence of fully knowing what might have worked for Tom and with the awareness that each and every case is different, I will attempt here to summarise the literature on suicidal ideation post-injury and the recommendations for practice.

Following on from the information provided in the National Suicide Prevention Strategy (2012), it is clear that substance misuse and mental health disturbance are common factors associated with an increased risk of suicide following TBI (Brenner, Homaifar, Adler, Wolfman & Kemp, 2009). While these two factors both increase overall risk, the combination of a premorbid history of both mental ill-health and substance misuse increases the risk of suicide by 21 times compared to those within the population who have no such history (Simpson & Tate, 2005). This is significant in a group already at a three times greater risk than the general population (Bahraini et al., 2013; Madsen et al., 2018).

As with the general population, hopelessness is also implicated as a risk factor for suicidality (Simpson & Tate, 2002, 2005). Given that this is a population of individuals who may well have lost many, if not all, aspects of their pre-injury lives, hopelessness is likely to be a common factor for many people. Couple this with an increased sense of social isolation that comes from having a reduced social support net-work following injury, due to personality changes and an inability to return to work (among many other factors), it is clear why this group may feel particularly hopeless. A further factor here may also be social deprivation, with many individuals post-injury struggling to gain access to welfare support or supported housing due to a lack of understanding of their disabilities (Odumuyiwa et al., 2019).

More recent literature has suggested that some individuals with TBI experience a sense of chronic suicidality post-injury. While their likeli-hood of engaging in suicidal ideation or attempts may be more transient in nature, underneath this is an enduring desire or impulse to end their own lives (Knight, Norman & Simpson, 2019). Periods of more intense suicidality, which lead to suicide attempts, is associated with specific triggers (such as pain and stressful life events), feeling trapped and having poor self-worth. Individuals within this study highlighted feelings of a lack of sense of self that had affected their overall self-worth. This was further exacerbated by a need to rely heavily on others and relying too heavily on risky coping behaviours such as alcohol or drug misuse (Knight et al., 2019). Sadly, this study also identified that an inability to physically carry out acts of suicide (due to physical disability) was a key factor in preventing suicide.

This paints a somewhat bleak picture for individuals who experi-ence suicidality post-injury, but the literature does also highlight key protective factors that can reduce suicidal ideation. Good levels of social support, hope and religion or spirituality can help to mediate these feelings of suicidality (Brenner et al., 2009; Knight et al., 2019), as can building one's own sense of self-worth (Knight et al., 2019). This identifies the importance of community rehabilitation and integration that focus on rebuilding the person's life post-injury and increasing their access to wider social networks. Access to commu-nity rehabilitation increases the likelihood that individuals will be able to return to some form of employment or education post-injury (Brannigan et al., 2017). This is an important component in building self-worth (Khan, Baguley & Cameron, 2003).

Community integration services can also be effective here at ensuring that people have a social support network post-injury, through engaging in social events or attending day centre services (Brown, Gordon & Spielman, 2003). These elements help to foster a sense of purpose that can increase self-esteem and self-worth (Brown et al., 2003), and in turn reduce suicidality (Brenner et al., 2009; Knight et al., 2019). Finally, it is important that while individuals have access to support networks, they also have a sense of independence and a degree of ownership over their lives so that they can grow their own self-worth (Knight et al., 2019). This, in turn, may lead to closer and more mutually beneficial support networks. Interestingly, the study by Knight et al. (2019) identified that a key protective factor against suicide was having a sense of the grief others would experience in the event of the person's death. This was particularly the case when the individual had children. By nurturing social networks, individuals may become more in tune with the feelings of those around them and become more acutely aware of their importance in the lives of others. This is likely to be significant in reducing the sense of hopelessness (Panzarella, Alloy & Whitehouse, 2006).

Final reflections

This is now the end of this book. At the time of writing it is 5 years and 3 months, almost to the day, since Tom took his own life. While the pain is less acute than it was 5 years ago, the sense of despair and loss at Tom's absence in my life has not disappeared. While discussing my conclusions to this book with a close friend we reflected on the kinds of things people say when someone experiences loss; that it will get easier, that time is a great healer and that life goes on. On reflection, the only one of these statements I feel is entirely true is that life does go on. It is inevitable that those left behind must continue with their lives. As such, there is a natural process of adjustment, learning to accommodate the absence of someone in one's life. But it does not get easier. What is easier for me is that I do not find myself thinking about Tom every minute of every day anymore, like I did when he first died. Some days I may not think about him at all, although these days are very rare. I have also learnt over time to think about him in a more positive light; remembering the funny times I had with him, his dark but fantastically attuned sense of humour, his surprisingly astute perspective on the world. I tend not to dwell so much on his death and his absence and instead try to view him as still being here in part, even though he is not physically with us anymore. But time has not healed the pain and his loss in my life has not become easier. On days when I allow myself to stop and contemplate what happened to Tom, and the things that led to his death, I still find myself rapidly brought to tears; a surge of emotion rises up inside me that desperately wants to be let out. Sadly, as life does go on, I have learnt to push those feelings down again and only occasionally let them out of their securely fastened box. Without this the pain and grief would be too debilitating to function day to day.

Tom was a man of contradiction. To those who knew him he was an oddity, eccentric, dysfunctional. At times he was difficult, aggressive, rude and quite smelly! But he was also incredibly intelligent and funny. He had the sharpest wit of anyone I have ever known and despite his fatalistic view of the world, he could sometimes say the funniest things. His humour is the thing I miss most about Tom. I miss his funny Christmas cards (on the front would say 'Jesus loves you' with a picture of Father Christmas and inside would say 'just as well because no other **** does') and rude but amusing t-shirts ('same s**t different day', 'I have a brain injury what's your excuse?'). I miss hearing him trundling through town in his wheelchair with his music blasting out of a stereo at top volume, beeping (with a lorry horn) at passers-by who did not get out of his way. I miss going to him and venting about family issues that were bothering me as he was the only one who was able to laugh it all off and help me gain perspective again. I miss seeing him wondering around in only a dressing gown (no pants!) or being dressed up with a top hat and tails, shining polished army boots and an old school tie. All these things hurt as much now as they did 5 years ago but I have learnt to keep them hidden and only express them when it is appropriate to do so. Sadly, as time goes on it feels less acceptable to do so. This is of course the same feeling anyone who has lost someone close to them will feel. When suicide is involved I think this can feel even more difficult as the stigma means people struggle with hearing this grief expressed openly. Writing this book has helped, as has the number of presentations I have done talking about Tom's life and death. But these talks are not focused on the person so much as a case study, as is this book in many ways. The personal story of who Tom was is something that even now I find difficult to discuss. Instead my focus has moved towards using Tom's story as a case study; trying to raise the awareness that is needed to ensure that other families and other individuals like Tom receive the support they so desperately need.

While Tom is unique in many ways, and there will never be anyone quite like him, he is not as unusual as many may think. The sad reality is that there are Toms in many cities and towns across the UK, and around the world. These are individuals who have experienced a brain injury, have been saved by the miracles of modern medicine and then discarded like an inconvenient blemish on society. Tom deserved so much more from the services that were meant to look after him and so do all the other Toms out there, and all those that are to come. As professionals we must start accepting that Tom is not an extreme and unusual case; he represents how a person's life can turn out following brain injury if they are not given access to the appropriate services and forms of support.

I hope that this book will serve as a useful reminder to professionals of the dangers of complacency when dealing with clients like Tom. I hope too that it will raise awareness of the importance of improved training for professionals working with those with brain injury; of improved access to community rehabilitation and integration services; of integrated case managed systems of support that provide specialist neuro-specific services; of improved safeguarding and risk management systems that accurately detect and heed warnings of risk; of the need for an increase in specific services that specialise in working with individuals with complex needs. Finally, I hope that this book serves as a comfort to other families who have been, or who are going, through similar situations. My story is not a comfort in the sense that it did not end well for Tom or us, but I hope that it will demonstrate to other families that they are not alone. That there are others out there who know what they are going through, who are thinking of them. This brings me to the final point of this book, the need for family support. While this book has told Tom's story, of his life, his injury and his death, it is my story too. It is Betty's story and Anna's story. It is the story of every family member who has had to endure the post-discharge battles following brain injury with limited or no service provision; left abandoned and out of their depth. There is woefully poor provision out there for individuals post-injury and as such they are a population of silent victims, which includes family members. Even when services are present we are the ones who remain (often entirely) silent, left in the dark, consigned to the back rooms, behind closed doors. We need recognition and we need to have our voices heard. In the end it is us who will be there day in and day out to support people like Tom. Therefore, it is us that need ongoing support in that journey. I hope that over time Tom's story will help to ensure a change in the way systems work, within the UK and internationally, and that Tom's legacy will be to save the lives of other individuals who otherwise may have lost their lives to suicide.

References

Adshead, C., Norman, A. & Holloway, M. (2019). The inter-relationship between acquired brain injury, substance use and homelessness; the impact of adverse childhood experiences: An interpretative phenomenological analysis study. *Disability & Rehabilitation*, 1–13. doi: 10.1080/09638288.2019.1700565

Bahraini, N. H., Simpson, G. K., Brenner, L. A., Hoffberg, A. S. & Schneider, A. L. (2013). Suicidal ideation and behaviours after traumatic brain injury: A systematic review. *Brain Impairment*, *14*, 92–112.

Bay, E. H., Bonnie, M., Williams, R. A., Kirsch, N. & Gillespie, B. (2002). Chronic stress, sense of belonging, and depression among survivors of traumatic brain injury. *Journal of Nursing Scholarship*, *34*, 221–226.

Bennett, D. (2018). Is executive dysfunction and poor insight following ABI reflected in the framework for defining capacity? (unpublished dissertation). University of Plymouth, Plymouth, Devon, UK.

Bessell, A. L., Watkins, E. R. & Williams, H. W. (2008). Depressive rumination reduces specificity of autobiographical memory recall in acquired brain injury. *Journal of the Neuropsychological Society*, *14*, 63–70.

Biddle, L. (2003). Public hazards or private tragedies? An exploratory study of the effect of coroners' procedures on those bereaved by suicide. *Social Science & Medicine*, *56*(5), 1033–1045.

Bombardier, C. H., Fann, J. R., Temkin, N. R., Essleman, P. C., Barber, J. & Dikmen, S. S. (2010). Rates of major depressive disorder and clinical outcomes following traumatic brain injury. *Journal of American Medical Association*, *303*(19), 1938–1945.

Boss, P. (1999). *Ambiguous loss: Learning to live with unresolved grief.* Cambridge, MA: Harvard University Press.

Boss, P. & Carnes, D. (2012). The myth of closure. *Family Process*, *51*, 456–469.

Bousman, C. A., Twanley, E. W., Vella, L., Gale, M., Everall, I. P. & Heaton, R. K. (2010). Homelessness and neuropsychological impairment: Preliminary analysis of adults entering outpatient psychiatric treatment. *The Journal of Nervous and Mental Disease*, *198*(11), 790–794.

Brannigan, C., Galvin, R., Walsh, M. E., Loughnane, C., Morrissey, E. J., Macey, C. & Horgan, N. F. (2017). Barriers and facilitators associated with return to work after stroke: A qualitative meta-synthesis. *Disability and Rehabilitation*, *39*(3), 211–222.

Brenner, L. A., Homaifar, B. Y., Adler, L. E., Wolfman, J. H. & Kemp, J. (2009). Suicidality and veterans with a history of traumatic brain injury: Precipitating events, protective factors, and prevention strategies. *Rehabilitation Psychology*, *54*(4), 390–397.

Brown, M., Gordon, W. A. & Spielman, L. (2003). Participation in social and recreational activity in the community by individuals with traumatic brain injury. *Rehabilitation Psychology*, *48*(4), 266.

Burridge, A. C., Williams, W. H., Yates, P., Harris, A. & Ward, C. (2007). Spousal relationship satisfaction following acquired brain injury: The role of insight and socio-emotional skill. *Neuropsychological Rehabilitation*, *17*(1), 95–105.

Byard, K. & Gosling, S. (2013). Re-writing the story of childhood brain injury: How systemic and narrative approaches help. *Article in Context*, 125.

Casey, B. J., Giedd, J. N. & Thomas, K. M. (2000). Structural and functional brain development and its relation to cognitive development. *Biological Psychology*, *54*(1–3), 241–257.

Catroppa, C., Hearps, S., Crossley, L., Yeates, K., Beauchamp, M., Fusella, J. & Anderson, V. (2017). Social and behavioral outcomes following childhood traumatic brain injury: What predicts outcome at 12 months post-insult? *Journal of Neurotrauma*, *34*(7), 1439–1447.

Clark-Wilson, J. & Holloway, M. (2019). *Family experience of brain injury: Saving, coping, adjusting* (1st ed.). Abingdon, UK: Routledge.

Corrigan, J. D. & Deutschle, J. J. (2008). The presence and impact of traumatic brain injury among clients in treatment for co-occurring mental illness and substance abuse. *Brain Injury*, *22*, 223–231.

Crosson, B., Barco, P. P., Velozo, C. A., Bolesta, M. M., Cooper, P. V., Werts, D. & Brobeck, T. C. (1989). Awareness and compensation in post-acute head injury rehabilitation. *Journal of Head Trauma Rehabilitation*, *4*, 46–54.

Department for Health and Social Care. (2012). *The National Suicide Prevention Stategy for England*. Department for Health and Social Care: London, UK.

Dyer, K. F., Bell, R., McCann, J. & Rauch, R. (2006). Aggression after traumatic brain injury: Analysing socially desirable responses and the nature of aggressive traits. *Brain Injury*, *20*(11), 1163–1173.

Engel, G. L. (1980). The clinical application of the biopsychosocial model. *The American Journal of Psychiatry*, *137*, 535–544.

Felde, A. B., Westermeyer, J. & Thuras, P. (2006). Co-morbid traumatic brain injury and substance disorder: Childhood predictors and adult correlates. *Brain Injury*, *20*(1), 41–49.

Felitti, V. J., Anda, R. F., Nordenberg, D., Williamson, D. F., Spitz, A., Edwards, V., Koss, M.P. & Marks, J.S. (1998). Relationship of childhood abuse and household dysfunction to many of the leading causes of death in adults: The Adverse Childhood Experiences (ACE) Study. *American Journal of Preventative Medicine, 14*(4), 245–258.

Fleminger, S. (2008). Long-term psychiatric disorders after traumatic brain injury. *European Journal of Anaesthesiology, 25*, 123–130.

Flynn, M. (2016). *The death of 'Tom' a serious case review.* Somerset, UK: Somerset Safeguarding Adults Board.

Fortener, R. G. (2000). *Relationship between work setting, client prognosis, suicide ideation, and burnout in psychologists and counselors* (Doctoral dissertation, ProQuest Information & Learning).

Garrouste-Orgeas, M., Perier, A., Mouricou, P., Gregoire, C., Bruel, C., Brochon, S., … Misset, B. (2014). Writing in and reading ICU diaries: Qualitative study of families' experience in the ICU. *PloS ONE, 9*(10), e110146. doi:10.1371/journal.pone.0110146

George, M. S. & Gilbert, S. (2018). Mental Capacity Act (2005) assessments: Why everyone needs to know about the frontal lobe paradox. *The Neuropsychologist, 5*, 59–66.

Gogtay, N., Giedd, J. N., Lusk, L., Hayashi, K. M., Greenstein, D., Vaituzis, A. C., … Rapoport, J. L. (2004). Dynamic mapping of human cortical development during childhood through early adulthood. *Proceedings of the National Academy of Sciences, 101*(21), 8174–8179.

Goranson, T. E., Graves, R. E., Allison, D. & Freniere, R. L. (2003). Community integration following multidisciplinary rehabilitation for traumatic brain injury. *Brain Injury, 17*(9), 759–774.

Gould, K. R., Ponsford, J. L., Johnston, L. & Schönberger, M. (2011). The nature, frequency and course of psychiatric disorders in the first year after traumatic brain injury: A prospective study. *Psychological Medicine, 41*(10), 2099–2109.

Graff, H., Christensen, U., Poulsen, I. & Egerod, I. (2017). Patient perspectives on navigating the field of traumatic brain injury rehabilitation: A qualitative thematic analysis. *Disability and Rehabilitation, 40*(8), 926–934. doi:10.1080/09638288.2017.1280542

Graham, D. P. & Cardon, A. L. (2008). An update on substance use and treatment following traumatic brain injury. *Annuals of the New York Academy of Science, 1141*, 148–162.

Griese, B., Burns, M. R., Farro, S. A., Silvern, L. & Talmi, A. (2017). Comprehensive grief care for children and families: Policy and practice implications. *American Journal of Orthopsychiatry, 87*(5), 540.

Griffin, J. M., Lee, M. K., Bangerter, L. R., Van Houtven, C. H., Friedemann-Sánchez, G., Phelan, S. M. & Meis, L. A. (2017). Burden and mental health among caregivers of veterans with traumatic brain injury/polytrauma. *American Journal of Orthopsychiatry, 87*(2), 139.

Headway UK. (2018a). *Statistics.* Nottingham: Author. Retrieved from www.headway.org.uk/about-brain-injury/further-information/statistics/

Headway UK. (2018b). *Right first time*. Nottingham: Author. Accessed 19.08.19. Retrieved from www.headway.org.uk/news-and-campaigns/cam paigns/right-first-time/

Hoffman, J. M., Pagulayan, K. F., Zawaideh, N., Dikmen, S., Temkin, N. & Bell, K. R. (2007). Understanding pain after traumatic brain injury. *American Journal of Physical Medicine Rehabilitation*, *86*(12), 962–969.

Holloway, M. (2014). How is ABI assessed and responded to in non-specialist settings? Is specialist education required for all social care professionals? *Social Care and Neurodisability*, *5*(4), 201–2013.

Holloway, M. & Fyson, R. (2015). Acquired brain injury, social work and the challenges of personalisation. *British Journal of Social Work*, *46*(5), 1301–1317.

Holloway, M., Orr, D. & Clark-Wilson, J. (2019). Experiences of challenges and support among family members of people with acquired brain injury: A qualitative study in the UK. *Brain Injury*, *33*(4), 401–411. doi:10.1080/02699052.2019.1566967

Horowitz, M. J., Siegel, B., Holen, A., Bonanno, G. A., Milbrath, C. & Stinson, C. H. (2003). Diagnostic criteria for complicated grief disorder. *Focus*, *1*(3), 290–298.

House of Lords. (2014). *Mental capacity act 2005: Post-legislative scrutiny*. London: The Stationary Office.

Hwang, S. W., Colantonio, A., Chiu, S., Tolomiczenko, G., Kiss, A., Cowan, L., Redelmeier, D.A. & Levinson, W. (2008). The effect of traumatic brain injury on the health of homeless people. *Canadian Medical Association Journal*, *179*(8), 779–784.

Ingelhard, I. M., McNally, R. J. & van Schie, K. (2019). Retrieving and modifying traumatic memories: Recent research relevant to the three controversies. *Current Directions in Psychological Science*, *28*(1), 91–96.

Jawaid, M. T., Amalnath, S. D. & Subrahmanyam, D. K. S. (2017). Neurological outcomes following suicidal hanging: A prospective study of 101 patients. *Annals of the Indian Academy of Neurology*, *20*(2), 106–108.

Jenkinson, A. & Chamberlain, J. (2019). How misinterpretation of 'unwise decisions' principle illustrates value of legal literacy for social workers. *Community Care*. Retrieved July 1, 2019, from www.communitycare.co.uk/2019/06/28/misinterpretation-unwise-decisions-principle-illustrates-value-legal-liter acy-social-workers/ Retrieved for reference 17th January 2020.

Jordan, J. & Linden, M. A. (2013). 'It's like a problem that doesn't exist': The emotional well-being of mothers caring for a child with brain injury. *Brain Injury*, *27*, 1063–1072.

Khan, F., Baguley, I. J. & Cameron, I. D. (2003). 4: Rehabilitation after traumatic brain injury. *Medical Journal of Australia*, *178*(6), 290–295.

Kim, H. & Colantonio, A. (2010). Effectiveness of rehabilitation in enhancing community integration after acute traumatic brain injury: A systematic review. *American Journal of Occupational Therapy*, *64*(5), 709–719.

Kissane, D. W. & Bloch, S. (1994). Family grief. *The British Journal of Psychiatry*, *164*(6), 728–740.

Knight, E. & Norman, A. (2017). *A qualitative assessment of the effectiveness of the Hospital Liaison Officer service*. Report to Headway UK. Plymouth, UK: Plymouth University.

Knight, E., Norman, A. & Simpson, G. (2019). Living with suicidality following traumatic brain injury: A qualitative study. *Brain Injury*, Submitted.

Kõlves, K., Zhao, Q., Ross, V., Hawgood, J., Spence, S. H. & De Leo, D. (2019). Suicide and other sudden death bereavement of immediate family members: An analysis of grief reactions six-months after death. *Journal of Affective Disorders*, *243*, 96–102.

Koponen, S., Taiminen, T., Portin, R., Himanen, L., Isoniemi, H., Heinonen, H., Hinkka, S. & Tenovuo, O. (2002). Axis I and II psychiatric disorders after traumatic Brain Injury: A 30 year follow-up study. *American Journal of Psychiatry*, *159*(8), 1315–1321.

Kreutzer, J. S., Rapport, L. J., Marwitz, J. H., Harrison-Felix, C., Hart, T., Glenn, M. & Hammond, F. (2009). Caregivers' well-being after traumatic brain injury: A multicenter prospective investigation. *Archives of Physical Medicine and Rehabilitation*, *90*(6), 939–946.

Langlois, J., Rutland-Brown, W., & Wald, M. (2006). The epidemiology and impact of traumatic brain injury. *Journal of Head Trauma Rehabilitation*, *21*, 375–378.

Leigh-Hunt, N., Bagguley, D., Bash, K., Turner, V., Turnbull, S., Valtorta, N. & Caan, W. (2017). An overview of systematic reviews on the public health consequences of social isolation and loneliness. *Public Health*, *152*, 157–171.

Linden, M. A. & Boylan, A. M. (2010). 'To be accepted as normal': Public understanding and misconceptions concerning survivors of brain injury. *Brain Injury*, *24*, 642–650.

Lingsma, H. F., Roozenbeek, B., Steyerberg, E. W., Murray, G. D. & Mass, A. I. R. (2010). Early prognosis in traumatic brain injury: From prophecies to predictions. *Lancet: Neurology*, *9*(5), 543–554.

Linley, P. A. (2003). Positive adaptation to trauma: Wisdom as both process and outcome. *Journal of Traumatic Stress*, *16*(6), 601–610.

Lynch, S. H. & Lobo, M. L. (2012). Compassion fatigue in family caregivers: A Wilsonian concept analysis. *Journal of Advanced Nursing*, *68*(9), 2125–2134.

Ma, Z., Bayley, M. T., Periier., L., Dhir, P., Depatie, L., Comper, P., ... Munce, S. E. P. (2017). The association between adverse childhood experiences and traumatic brain injury/concussion in adulthood: A scoping review protocol. *BMJ Open*, *7*(10), e018425.

Maas, A. R., Menon, D., Adelson, D., Andelic, N., Bell, M. J. & Yaffe, Y. (2017). Traumatic brain injury: Integrated approaches to improve prevention, clinical care, and research. *Lancet Neurology*. doi:10.1016/S1474-4422(17)30371-X

Mackelprang, J. L., Harpin, S. B., Grubenhoff, J. A. & Rivara, F. P. (2014). Adverse outcomes among homeless adolescents and young adults who report a history of traumatic brain injury. *American Journal of Public Health*, *104*(10), 1986–1992.

Madsen, T., Erlangsen, A. & Orlovska, S. (2018). Association between traumatic brain injury and risk of suicide. *JAMA*, *320*(6), 580–588.

Mainio, A., Kyllönen, T., Viilo, K., Hakko, H., Särkioja, T. & Räsänen, P. (2007). Traumatic brain injury, psychiatric disorders and suicide: A population-based study of suicide victims during the years 1988–2004 in Northern Finland. *Brain Injury*, *21*(8), 851–855.

Manuel, J., Crowe, M., Inder, M. & Henaghan, M. (2018). Suicide prevention in mental health services: A qualitative analysis of coroners' reports. *International Journal of Mental Health Nursing*, *27*(2), 642–651.

Moore, S., Wotus, R., Norman, A., Holloway, M. & Dean, J. (2019). Cloak of Competence: Brain injury and mental capacity legislation. *Journal of Adult Protection*, *21*(4), 201–218.

Nampiaparampil, D. E. (2008). Prevalence of chronic pain after traumatic brain injury: A systematic review. *Journal of American Medical Association*, *300*(6), 711–719.

Niederhoffer, K. G. & Pennebaker, J. W. (2002). Sharing one's story: On the benefits of writing or talking about emotional experience. In C. R. Snyder & S. J. Lopez (Eds.), *Handbook of positive psychology* (pp. 573–583). New York: Oxford University Press.

Norman, A. (2016). A preventable death? A family's perspective on an adult safeguarding review regarding an adult with traumatic brain injury". *The Journal of Adult Protection*, *18*(6), 341–352. doi:10.1108/JAP-08-2016-0017

Oddy, M. & Da Silva Ramos, S. (2013). The clinical and cost-benefits of investing in neurobehavioural rehabilitation: A multi-centre study. *Brain Injury*, *27*, 1500–1507.

Oddy, M., Moir, J. F., Fortesque, D. & Chadwick, S. (2012). The prevalence of traumatic brain injury in the homeless community in a UK city. *Brain Injury*, *26*(9), 1058–1064.

Odumuyiwa, T., Kennedy, M., Norman, A., Holloway, M., Suffield, F., Forrest, H. & Dick, H. (2019). Improving access to social care services following Acquired Brain Injury: A needs analysis. *Journal of Long Term Care*. 2019, 164–179.

Orff, H. J., Ayalon, L. & Drummond, S. P. (2009). Traumatic brain injury and sleep disturbance: A review of current research. *The Journal of Head Trauma Rehabilitation*, *24*(3), 155–165.

Panzarella, C., Alloy, L. B. & Whitehouse, W. G. (2006). Expanded hopelessness theory of depression: On the mechanisms by which social support protects against depression. *Cognitive Therapy and Research*, *30*(3), 307–333.

Papalimperi, A. H., Athanaselis, S. A., Mina, A. D., Papoutsis, I. I., Spiliopoulou, C. A. & Papadodima, S. A. (2019). Incidence of fatalities of road traffic accidents associated with alcohol consumption and the use of psycho-active drugs: A 7-year survey (2011–2017). *Experimental and Therapeutic Medicine, 18*(3), 2299–2306.

Parry-Jones, B. L., Vaughan, F. L. & Cox, W. M. (2004). Traumatic brain injury and substance misuse: A systematic review of prevalence and outcomes research (1994–2004). *Neuropsychological Rehabilitation, 16*(5), 537–560.

Parson, K. (2015). Care Act right to advocacy being undermined by chaotic commissioning and lack of resources. Community Care. Retrieved from www.communitycare.co.uk/2015/08/03/care-act-right-advocacy-undermined-chaotic-commissioning-lack-resources/ Retrieved 17ᵗʰ Janauary 2020.

Parsonage, M. (2016). *Traumatic brain injury: An economic analysis.* London, UK: Centre for mental health.

Peters, K., Cunningham, C., Murphy, G. & Jackson, D. (2016). Helpful and unhelpful responses after suicide: Experiences of bereaved family members. *International Journal of Mental Health Nursing, 25*(5), 418–425.

Petersen, H. & Sanders, S. (2015). Caregiving and Traumatic Brain Injury: Coping with grief and loss. *Health and Social Work, 40*(4), 325–328.

Piccenna, L., Lanninun, N. A., Gruen, R., Pattuwage, L. & Bragge, P. (2016). The experience of discharge for patients with an acquired brain injury from the inpatient to the community setting: A qualitative review. *Brain Injury, 30*, 241–251.

Ponsford, J., Whelan-Goodinson, R. & Bahar-Fuchs, A. (2007). Alcohol and drug use following traumatic brain injury: A prospective study. *Brain Injury, 21*(13–14), 1385–1392.

Ponsford, J. & Schönberger, M. (2010). Family functioning and emotional state two and five years after traumatic brain injury. *Journal of the International Neuropsychological Society, 16*(2), 306–312.

Salter, K., Foley, N., Jutai, J., Bayley, M. & Teasell, R. (2008). Assessment of community integration following rehabilitation for traumatic brain injury. *Brain Injury, 22*, 820–835.

Sanders, C. M. (1980). A comparison of adult bereavement in the death of a spouse, child, and parent. *OMEGA-Journal of Death and Dying, 10*(4), 303–322.

Sariaslan, A., Sharp, D. J., D'Onofrio, B. M., Larsson, H. & Fazel, S. (2016). Long term outcomes associated with traumatic brain injury in childhood and adolescence: A nationwide Swedish cohort study of a wide range of medical and social outcomes. *PLoS Med, 13*(8), e1002103.

Savage, R. (2010). *Brain development in children and adolescents: What happens after brain injury?* Youngsville, NC: Lash and Associates Publishing.

Schauer, M. & Elbert, T. (2015). Dissociation following traumatic stress: Etiology and treatment. *Journal of Psychology, 218*, 109–127.

Schmidt, M. & Azoulay, E. (2012). Having a loved one in the ICU: The forgotten family. *Current Opinions in Critical Care, 18*(5), 540–547.

Sheehan, L. L., Corrigan, P. W., Al-Khouja, M. A. & Stigma of Suicide Research Team. (2017). Stakeholder perspectives on the stigma of suicide attempt survivors. *Crisis*, *38*(**2**), 73–81.

Shields, C., Kavanagh, M. & Russo, K. (2017). A qualitative systematic review of the bereavement process following suicide. *OMEGA-Journal of Death and Dying*, *74*(4), 426–454.

Shiroma, E. J., Ferguson, P. L. & Pickelsimer, E. E. (2012). Prevalence of traumatic brain injury in an offender population: A metaanalysis. *Journal of Head Trauma Rehabilitation*, *27*(3), e1–e10.

Silver, J. M., McAllister, T. W., & Arciniegas, D. B. (Eds.). (2018). *Textbook of traumatic brain injury*. American Psychiatric Pub.

Simpson, G. & Tate, R. (2002). Suicidality after traumatic injury: Demographic, injury and clinical correlates. *Psychological Medicine*, *32*(4), 687–697.

Simpson, G. & Tate, R. (2005). Clinical features of suicide attempts after traumatic brain injury. *The Journal of Nervous and Mental Disease*, *193*(10), 680–685.

Sinnakaruppan, I. & Williams, D. M. (2001). Family carers and the adult head-injured: A critical review of carers' needs. *Brain Injury*, *15*, 653–672.

Stonnington, H. H. (1997). Editorial: Community based rehabilitation. *Brain Injury*, *11*, 155.

Thomas, M. (2011). Reflections on community-based rehabilitation. *Psychology and Developing Societies*, *23*(2), 277–291.

Thompson, M. P., Kingree, J. B. & Lamis, D. (2019). Associations of adverse childhood experiences and suicidal behaviors in adulthood in a U.S. nationally representative sample. *Child Care Health and Development*, *45*(1), 121–128.

Townshend, J. & Norman, A. (2018). The secondary impact of traumatic brain injury: An interpretative phenomenological analysis of the experiences of family and friends. *The Family Journal*, *26*, 77–85.

Turner, B., Fleming, J., Parry, J., Vromans, M., Cornwell, P., Gordon, C. & Ownsworth, T. (2010). Caregivers of adults with traumatic brain injury: The emotional impact of transition from hospital to home. *Brain Impairment*, *11*(3), 281–292.

Turner-Stokes, L. (2008). Evidence for the effectiveness of multi-disciplinary rehabilitation following acquired brain injury: A synthesis of two systematic approaches. *Journal of Rehabilitation Medicine*, *40*, 691–701.

UKABIF (2018). *Acquired brain injury and neurorehabilitation time for change: All party parliamentary group on acquired brain injury report*. London, UK: UKABIF.

Van Velzen, J. M., van Bennekom, C. A. M., Edelaar, M. J. A. & Sluiter, J. K. (2009). Frings-Dresen. How many people return to work after acquired brain injury? A systematic review. *Brain Injury*, *23*(6), 473–488.

Walker, R., Cole, J. E., Logan, T. K. & Corrigan, J. D. (2007). Screening substance abuse treatment clients for traumatic brain injury: Prevalence and characteristics. *Journal of Head Trauma Rehabilitation*, *22*(6), 360–367.

Weil, Z. M., Corrigan, J. D. & Karelina, K. (2016). Alcohol abuse after traumatic brain injury: Experimental and clinical evidence. *Neuroscience and Behavioural Reviews, 62*, 89–99.

Wiebe, D. J., Cornstock, R. D. & Nance, M. L. (2011). Concussion research: A public health priority. *Injury Prevention, 17*(1). doi:10.1136/ip.2010.031211

Williams, W. H., Mewse, A. J., Tonks, J., Mills, S., Burgess, C. N. & Cordan, G. (2010). Traumatic brain injury in a prison population: Prevalence and risk for re-offending. *Brain Injury, 24*(10), 1184–1188.

Wood, R. L. & Yurakul, L. K. (1997). Change in relationship status following traumatic brain injury. *Brain Injury, 11*, 491–502.

Wright, J. & Chung, M. C. (2001). Mastery or mystery? Therapeutic writing: A review of the literature. *British Journal of Guidance & Counselling, 29*(3), 277–291.

Index

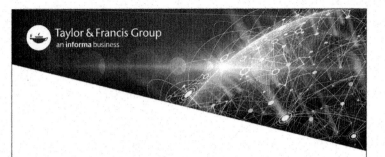